Cultural Vistas and Sites of Identity

Essays on Literature, Film and American Studies

Réka M. Cristian

©2014 Réka M. Cristian
©2014 Szeged, AMERICANA eBooks

General editors: Réka M. Cristian & Zoltán Dragon

ISBN: 978-615-5423-01-7

AMERICANA eBooks is a division of *AMERICANA – E-Journal of American
Studies in Hungary*, published by the Department of American Studies,
University of Szeged, Hungary.
http://ebooks.americanaejournal.hu

Cover photograph by Anna Fenyvesi
Book design by Zoltán Dragon

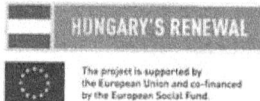

HUNGARY'S RENEWAL

The project is supported by
the European Union and co-financed
by the European Social Fund.

The publication of this book was supported by Project TÁMOP - 4.2.1/B -
09/1/KONV – 2010 - 0005 – Creating the Center of Excellence at the University
of Szeged, supported by the European Union and co-financed by the European
Social Fund.

Printed in the United States of America

To my parents,
Réka and András Cristian

CONTENTS

Acknowledgements

The publication of this e-book[1] was supported by Project TÁMOP -
4.2.1/B - 09/1/KONV – 2010 - 0005 – Creating the Center of Excellence
at the University of Szeged, supported by the European Union and co-
financed by the European Social Fund.

Earlier versions of the essays that comprise this volume appeared in the
following places: "The Road Now Taken: American Studies: American
Studies in Hungary and Romania," in *Conference on British and American
Studies: Global Homogeneity, Local Identity*, gen. ed. Marinela Burada,
Transilvania University Press, Braşov, 2010, 11-24; "American Studies in
the Age of Visual/Electronic Reproduction," (co-authored with Zoltán
Dragon), in *Americana*, Vol. I. Nr.1, 2005, Website: http://primus.arts.u-
szeged.hu/american/americana/crmdz.htm; "Identity at Thresholds and
American Dramatic Frames: Paula Vogel's *How I Learned to Drive* and Ed-
ward Albee's *The Goat or Who Is Sylvia?*," in *Focus. Papers in English Literary
and Cultural Studies. Special Issue on American Studies: Frontiers, Borderlines, and
Frames*, ed. Gabriella Vöő, Pécs: Department of English Literatures and
Cultures, University of Pécs, 2007, 166-176; "Borderlands: Postcolonial
Identities in Contemporary American Literature.," in *Theory and Practice 4:
Proceedings from the Eight Conference of English, American and Canadian Studies
(Literature and Cultural Studies)*, ed. Jan Chovanec, Brno: Masaryk University,
2005, 35-42; "Ismét Frida Kahlo." [Frida Kahlo Revisited] Trans. Zoltán
Dragon, in *Filmkultúra*. 2004, Website: http://www.filmkultura.hu/regi/

---

[1] This book was originally released in e-book formats (prc and epub, available on
the site of the publisher at http://ebooks.americanaejournal.hu/books/cultural-
vistas-and-sites-of-identity), hence all the references to the text are preserved in this
version to match the digital edition.

2004/articles/essays/frida.hu.html; "Culturas de Identidad: Las imágenes en movimieinto de Frida Kahlo" [Cultures of Identity: Images in *Frida*] Trans. Servando Ortoll, in *Estudios sobre las Culturas Contemporáneas. Programa cultura. Revista de investigation y análisis*. Colima, Mexico: Universidad de Colima, Centro Universitario de Investigationes Sociales, Época II., Vol.XII., Núm. 24, diciembre 2006, 101-118; "The Roman Springs of Mrs. Stone: Auteurship in Tennessee Williams's Novel Adaptations." in *BAS* [*British and American Studies*] *2007*, ed. Hortensia Pârlog. Timişoara: Editura Universităţii de Vest, 2007, 87-96; "Play It Again Edward or Who Is Afraid to Adapt Albee?," in *Kultúrán innen és túl. Írások Rozsnyai Bálint tiszteletére/Within and Without Culture. Essays in Honor of Bálint Rozsnyai*, ed. Zoltán Vajda, Szeged: JATEPress, 2009, 83-95; "Transnational Negotiations in Alejandro González Iñárritu's *Babel*," in *Negotiations. An International Journal of Literary and Cultural Studies*, Vol. 1, March 2011, Ashis Sengupta and Ranjan Gosh, eds., Siliguri, Darjeeling: Registrar of the University of North Bengal, 27-38. I am grateful to the publishers for permission to include their copyright material in this e-book.

I wish to convey my thanks to Ruth Winterbottom Peacock for her precious company, witty comments and editorial acumen that helped me refine my essays into their current form and to Von Peacock for showing me the world of rare birds. I am most grateful to Gladys and Glenn "Gabby" Baker from Atlanta, Georgia, and to Enikő and Edward Jordan from Pocatello, Idaho, whose generous friendship fostered my earliest Americanist endeavors. Special thanks to Servando Ortoll for his remarkable translations of my texts into Spanish and to Zoltán Dragon, my closest colleague and friend for his share in the work and joy of the *AMERICANA* publications. I am especially grateful to Enikő Bollobás, whose friendship, encouragement and intellectual support helped me in various ways. I owe a special debt to the generosity of Liliana Hamzea, Pia Brînzeu and Ashis Sengupta in academic matters and to Avital Bloch, a close friend so far away. Above and beyond, I would like to convey my deepest gratitude to my husband, Róbert Túri, for his loving support and humor.

1. Introduction. The Road Now Taken: Cultural Vistas in American Studies

The joy of American studies is precisely in its lack of firm limits and borders.
Patricia Nelson Limerick

In this time of deep political division, national paranoia, and global uncertainty, scholars of the humanities, arts, and social sciences across the globe must learn from each other, share perspectives, and continue to broaden the range of ideas needed to bring about change.
Emory Elliott

Hungarian higher education has witnessed substantial changes since the fall of the Iron Curtain in 1989. During the intervening two decades these changes have had a considerable impact on all areas of research and practice with special regard to the Humanities in general and to the reception, development and study of American studies in particular. To understand the current issues of local American studies one needs to briefly contextualize the state of this complex interdisciplinary field at the regional and national level, and anchor these studies in the current global, transnational practices of the discipline.

American studies in Hungary—and in East-Central Europe—played a special role during the Cold War: the discipline, as Enikő Bollobás writes, was considered a "subversive field" of study and its teaching a "subversive enterprise" (563). The mission of East-Central European scholars of American studies is, Bollobás continues, first to "verify—in a post-communist and post-Cold War environment—the existence of an American Civilization by 'importing America (to pun on Richard Horowitz's expression)' into

1

their own culture" and second, to be "instrumental in the *kind* of civilization they *produce*" (577) by disseminating "advanced ideas in an intellectual
environment that did not itself produce them" while testing them in given
"historical, social, and cultural contexts" (578).

Hungarian American studies started with the work of László Országh
(1907-1984). As Zoltán Abádi-Nagy points out, Országh is the author of
several internationally pioneering books, among them, *Az amerikai
irodalomtörténetírás fejlődése* [*The Evolution of American Literary History*] published
in 1935, the first comprehensive history of American literature published in
Hungarian entitled *Az amerikai irodalom története* [*The History of American Literature*] (1967), and the first introduction to American studies in Hungary,
Bevezetés az amerikanisztikába (1972) ("Anglisztika-amerikanisztika a mai Magyarországon" 15). Furthermore, Országh founded the prestigious journal
Hungarian Studies in English (*HSE*), which he edited between 1963 and 1973.
During the 1960s, Országh, a pioneer in higher education, too, launched
American studies in the Hungarian university system at Lajos Kossuth University, the predecessor of the University of Debrecen, which today hosts
the North American Department of the Institute of English and American
Studies (see the webpage of the department at http://ieas.unideb.hu
/index.php?p=92).

At the beginning of the 1990s, Hungarian higher education witnessed a
proliferation of American studies departments. As Abádi-Nagy writes, the
Department of American Studies of Eötvös Loránd University in Budapest,
currently part of the School of English and American Studies, was founded
as an independent program in 1990 and received academic accreditation in
1994 (see http://das.elte.hu); the American Studies Department of Károly
Eszterházy Teacher's Training College in Eger (see http://www.ektf.hu/
~amerikanisztika) was also founded in 1990 ("Anglisztika-amerikanisztika a
mai Magyarországon" 17). The Department of American Studies of the
University of Szeged was also the product of the departmental boom of the
early 1990s, when it became an independent, full-value degree program,
today part of the Institute of English and American Studies of the University of Szeged (see the department's webpage at http://amerikanisztika.ieas-
szeged.hu). Additionally, a wide array of courses in American studies are
currently taught at other universities and colleges (University of Pécs, in
Veszprém, Nyíregyháza, Szombathely, etc.), mostly within the realm of
English.

The leading journal of English and American studies in Hungary, *Hungarian Journal of English and American Studies* (*HJEAS*, published since 1995
by the Institute of English and American Studies, University of Debrecen),
evolved out of the *Hungarian Studies in English* (*HSE*, first published in
1963). Abádi-Nagy pointed out in the "Editorial Note" of the first semi-
annual *HJEAS* issue that *HSE* issues were "the only undisrupted periodical

sequence devoted exclusively to English and American Studies" in the country, emphasizing that the successor, *HJEAS*, became "the senior Central European journal of English and American Studies" with issues "devoted exclusively to English and American Studies" determined to "respond to the new situation created in the wake of the vast social changes that took place in 1989 in Hungary" (1995). In a comprehensive survey of contemporary journal publishing in American studies, P. Giles and R. J. Ellis emphasized that *HJEAS* has "deliberately exploited its liminal geographical positions between Eastern and Western Europe, in the shadow of the old Austro-Hungarian empire," becoming a crucial publication articulating many important "counternarratives on behalf of not just Hungary but Central Europe more generally" (1046).

The *HJEAS* and the conference proceedings issued by the HUSSE (Hungarian Society for the Study of English) are the main sites of publications in the field alongside an increasing number of topics related to American studies featured in a number of other important Hungarian periodicals, mentioned by Abádi-Nagy in his 2009 survey of the state of the discipline in Hungary: *Eger Journal of American Studies* (published by Károly Eszterházy Teacher's Training College), *Epona* and *Focus* (University of Pécs), *Papers in English and American Studies* (University of Szeged), *Pázmány Papers in English and American Studies* (Pázmány Péter Catholic University), *Studies in English and American* and *The AnaChronist* (Eötvös Loránd University) ("Anglisztika-amerikanisztika a mai Magyarországon" 20-21). Moreover, the Hungarian Association for American Studies (HAAS), currently with a considerable number of members, was established in 1992 and has been a member of the European Association for American Studies (EAAS) since 1994.

In *The Futures of American Studies*, John Carlos Rowe suggested that one must act locally while thinking on a wider, global level by balancing national and international aims with different local interests and institutional configurations inside and outside the academia (171, 177). Hungarian American studies is following this scheme. Between 1989 and 1993, Hungarian English and American studies went through what Abádi-Nagy called the "early-phase-post-communist" period, followed and a "post-early-phase post-communist" period ("Anglisztika-amerikanisztika a mai Magyarországon" 13), which ended with Hungary's adheration to the Bologna Process. Today, American studies, integral part of the structures of the European Bologna Process signed by Hungary in 1999 and applied to our higher education since 2006, is on its way to achieve the above-mentioned balance by situating itself, to paraphrase Robert Frost's words, on a road under construction, "less traveled by" that envisages the synchronization of our present and future work in which the human and the technical aspects are creatively combined within digital humanities.

3

Since its outset, the American studies program in Szeged—my own university—has promoted, similar to other Hungarian American studies centers, particular dynamics in understanding American culture(s) by taking into account various interacting factors. These interactions, as Mel van Elteren observed in his study on Americanization outside the U.S., are meaningful encounters involving intricate processes of transculturation that effect a "differentiated view on the mediating processes involved in the appropriations of American exemplars and imports by local recipients" and inform a specific conceptualization that enables scholars, researchers and students "to capture relevant processes at the transnational level from a non-state-centered perspective" (365) by adapting them to their own critical practices. Informed by the above-mentioned approaches to the study of the field, in tandem adopting new media practices, the open access *AMERICANA E-Journal of American Studies in Hungary* (see http://americanaejournal.hu) published since 2005 by the Department of American Studies from the University of Szeged, alongside with its division, *AMERICANA eBooks* (see http://ebooks.americanaejournal.hu), provides a wide digital forum for scholars and students having interest in the field(s) of American studies in Hungary and abroad.

Recently, one of the most intriguing experiments concerning the direct involvement of the new media within the field of humanities was "Hacking the Academy. A Book Crowdsourced in One Week, a one-week project that took place between May 21-28, 2010 initiated by the Roy Rosenzweig Center for History and New Media at George Mason University" (see http://hackingtheacademy.org), which was immediately compiled into an open access volume edited by Dan Cohen and Tom Scheinfeldt. This project explored and presented the ways in which digital media and technology can revolutionize the academy and its disciplines through the playful "hacker ethos" (Suiter in Cohen and Scheinfeldt 2010) of its 177 contributors. In line with the democratic practice of *Hacking the Academy*, the use of new media in our current practice of American studies, combined with more collaborative modes of teaching and research aims to enhance the interactive inclusion of more unconventional histories of the non-canonized cultural paradigms that have been treated, as the editors wrote in the inaugural issue of the *AMERICANA E-Journal of American Studies in Hungary*, as naive or amateur texts, images, objects, sounds, events within previous institutionalized frames of the field (2005).

Certain roads have been taken in the practice of this relatively young field of study in the United States and all over the world, and many wait to be traveled especially in the digital   realm; the tendency today is toward comparative, idiosyncratic ways of understanding American culture(s) through synergic, transnational dialogues. Alan B. Howard, one of the earliest advocates of the use of new technologies in the field of American studies, observed that new technologies offer "a real and authentic challenge" to the field dominated mostly by the paradigm of the print because they represent "a genuine new force in the world, not just a rhetorical one" (1999). The employment of new technologies, he stressed, will allow practitioners "no *retreat to our disciplinary havens*" pushing us toward re-organizing not only "the way we think about our field, the way we do research and analysis, the way we think about our disciplinary and institutional objectives" (1999). In this new context, we, as scholars of a field continuously redefining itself, need to do our work more visibly: this can be achieved mostly by the new media tools that open up further spaces of cultural encounters for a broader, non-academic audience and can have impact, as Howard pointed out, "on public discussions and public understanding of the nature of American Culture" (1999). Thus the combination of novel technologies and the new media become indispensable tools in the practice of the discipline where teachers, researchers and students can become practical Emersonian New "American Scholars" and use their work to point what James Farrell called "the moral ecology of everyday life" (195).

In the light of the transnational turn and global technologies, New American studies today makes intensive use of the new media, which has become an indispensable tool in the practice of humanities. As Donald Pease observed, currently, an increasing number of scholars solicit the shift of the "wholesale configuration" (268) of the objects of American studies into various interdisciplinary formations by introducing "alternative politics of power and knowledge (267), but they seem to forget the powerful agency of the new media in this process. Matthias Oppermann noted that these processes of cultural reproduction, negotiation, contestation and critique, along with the most "cultural translations and appropriation currently under way have direct implication for the concepts and categories that constitute the interpretive frameworks" of New American studies where several categories "are undergoing substantial reconfiguration and call for a redefinition in the light of the new media" (346).

New media can also be instrumental in the implementation of other useful interdisciplinary encounters such as the "intercomprehesion" strategies. This new term was defined by Maria Filomena Capucho as the "co-construction of meaning in intercultural and interlinguistic contexts" (3) applied as an innovative methodology to enhance plurilingual competency within the multilingual context of the European Union communities (vs. the English as lingua franca). A term under permanent redefinition in the past two decades and mostly used in the linguistics contexts so far, intercomprehension shares common features with that of American studies. The application of this new form of communication "in which his individual uses his or her own language but yet understands that of the other" (3) can posit, both in cultural and linguistic sense within the transnational realm of

New American studies, a viable a model for more accurate cultural translations that could further expand the field's increasingly dialogic nature.

American studies has been undergoing continuous changes since its emergence in the 1930s as a field of study in the United States. A wide cultural enterprise still under construction, the discipline finds itself in a creative state of permanent crisis and is, according to Linda Kerber, engaged in a continuous redefinition of its subject(s) and of itself (419) in the United States and abroad.

The beginnings of the American studies as a distinct discipline date back to the 1930s when the first so-called American Civilization courses were introduced at Yale, George Washington, Harvard, Pennsylvania, and Smith, continuing in the 1940 and 1950s with more American Civilization programs in several other universities that, according to Kerber, offered "students enormous freedom to construct their own curricula," which, in turn, enabled them to innovate their studies so as to fit their own personal academic career (417). Today, fewer and fewer American colleges and universities have separate American studies programs; some run it as an interdepartmental program and some have post-gradual degrees under the label of American Civilization or History of American Civilization, or have no American studies program at all while an increasing number of American studies programs have opened outside the U.S. especially during the last twenty years.

The first main Americanist forum was the American Studies Association, founded in 1951, the oldest and the largest association devoted to the interdisciplinary study of American culture and history in the United States in tandem with the *American Quarterly* as ASA's premier academic journal. Today the internationalization of the discipline is reflected not only by the new methods of inquiry but also by the establishment of related associations and publications, such as the International American Studies Association (IASA) founded in 2000, the publication of *Comparative American Studies: An International Journal* (CAS) three years later, and the *Review of International American Studies* (RIAS) online journal first issued in 2006. The open access online academic *Journal of Transnational American Studies* (JTAS) released in 2009, among many other currently bourgeoning national and international publications, also rank the discipline as a transnational locus of knowledge, currently dwelling in an increasing number of official sites worldwide.

In 1999, the journal *American Studies International* published an intriguing compilation of talks by several American studies scholars presented at the 1998 Seattle Conference of the American Studies Association (ASA) entitled "Roundtables: The Imagined Community of International American Studies," which presented a bird's eye view on the situation of the discipline at the end of the 1990s in each participant's country. These scholars, among them Bruce Tucker, formulated crucial questions concerning the condition of this "intellectual borderland" (22) at the turn of the century in New Zealand, the United States of America, Canada, Japan and Turkey, and offered possible solutions to existing difficulties occurring in the practice of the discipline.

Maureen Montgomery from New Zealand set the agenda by espousing the idea of an international American studies community. Montgomery stressed the need to accomplish a genuine internationalization of the discipline by promoting the work of non-US based, foreign Americanists from diverse countries. Practicing in different locations outside the United States, these foreign teachers and researchers would contribute to the US-based scholarly community's mainstream scholarly practices that were primarily "radiating out from the United States" by encouraging cross-cultural analysis and challenging the dominant paradigms of the field "generated from within the United States" (5, 6, 7). Brenda Dixon-Gottschild, the U.S. participant, perceived American studies as a terrain that should embrace dissent rather than consensus in order to influence solutions; for her this field is a creative crossroads of interdisciplinary encounters on which she positions her own scholarship and research (9), as an individual enterprise among many others from Montgomery's "utopian" (7) imagined global community of American studies scholars.

Gönül Pultar's insightful contribution depicted a special Americanist position emerging from a non-Christian, non-Western environment. In Turkey, he emphasized, American studies represented mostly a means of exercising discourses of freedom because it enhanced the "possibility of doing 'new things' in a manner" that was not, at that time, "possible in other disciplines" (12) in the country's universities. Pultar praised the innovative force of new interdisciplinary methodologies in the field of the international American studies community and put forth the need to change Turkish institutional rigidity (14) together with the outdated configuration of these studies within the "patriarchal, authoritative, [and] hierarchical" (13) academic set-ups that obstructed the natural development of the discipline (14) in his country.

Although Japan and the United States have, as Hiroko Sato claims, been closely "connected politically, economically and culturally" (15), the skeptical attitude towards "imperialistic" attempts to disseminate American culture in Japan, especially through mass media and journalistic writings, sided by a historically coded "timidity" regarding the involvement in current political issues concerning the United States, resulted in the establishment of only two centers of American studies in Japan. Sato highlighted that, in this context, the practice of the discipline was mostly "limited to historical studies of American culture and society (16), a condition that called for urgent revision. This, she stressed, can be achieved through the involvement of "other practitioners of analysis and commentary on America" who could join the scholars in the field by asking what meaning does this discipline have to the Japanese people and what is the meaning of undertaking American studies in Japan (16) in an active dialogue that can be best reached by frequent exchanges of faculty and students throughout the international American studies community.

In talking about the institutionalization of the field in Canada, Tucker observed that there was a relatively small number of American studies programs in the country with no systematic work on the development of this discipline yet. He saw this situation as an outcome of both Canadian and American cultures, which are "inventions" themselves "constantly being reimagined" with a tendency to go beyond the standard nation state comparisons (21). To solve this problem, Tucker envisaged the idea of the "intellectual borderland" in which reciprocal relations among the practitioners of the field enhance mutual understanding of "the imagining that created the otherness" (22) they seek to continuously comprehend. In this intellectual borderland, besides acquiring new information about another place and culture, the practitioner also learns to transform her or his own understanding towards people and cultures through creative interaction. This transformation, however, is rather a reflection about "how we see" and "what the comparative act of seeing tells us about our past" (22) and present.

Similar to the roundtable of "The Imagined Community of International American Studies," other roundtables and talks held at various American studies forums featured the importance of new strategies in de-centered "readings" of America both from the United States and abroad. In the 2002 Presidential Address to the American Studies Association, Stephen Sumida reiterated the need for a genuine internationalization of the field—as previously articulated by Paul Lauter, Alice Kessler-Harris and Emory Elliott—by stressing that American studies is internationally performed by scholars "indigenous to their nations or their nations of origin" (351) whose contributions are imperative for the development of the field. Two years later, the internationalization of the field took another step forward. In her Presidential Address to the ASA, Shelley Fisher Fishkin inaugurated the "transnational turn" in American studies and highlighted the paramount importance of "collaboration across the borders" which helps "to improve and build on existing institutional structures" ("Crossroads of Cultures" 39). Here Fishkin also observed that "[o]utside the United States" the field is "sometimes constructed as being centered on the social sciences—economics, politics, foreign relations—while inside the United States it is dominated by the humanities" (42). Furthermore, outside the United States, students pursue American studies generally as a "shrewd career move that will help them succeed economically in their own country" while in the United States students tend to study this field "to develop critical analyses of American culture and society" (42).

Whatever the aim of pursuing these studies might be, it seems that the transnational turn is a road now taken with more new paradigms to discover and work with. In her "Response and Proposal" to the Symposium and roundtable discussion on "Redefinition of Citizenship and Revisions of Cosmopolitanism—Transnational Perspectives" (with Günter Lenz, Rob Kroes, Rüdiger Kunow, Alfred Hornung and William Boelhower as roundtable contributors) about the perspectives and dynamics of new cosmopolitanism, Fishkin proposed the introduction of the Digital Palimpsest Mapping Project (DPMP or Deep Maps), a collaborative work-in-progress digital project that highlights the "interdependence" of each practitioner as scholar, as citizen, and as human being (7) within what she coined as the "Transnational American Studies 2.0" (6). This "gateway" project aims to foster an open access archive of texts, events and phenomena (7) with a palimpsest of comments that would enable this open-ended endeavor to display the work and research of scholars and students working with topics pertaining to current New American studies.

In line with the transnational turn, the most intriguing reflections come from the New American studies practitioners from outside the United States of America. It is highly revealing to see the modes and the ways in which most academic interpretive communities, for example that of European practitioners of New American studies deal today with the expanding field of the discipline. The most comprehensive electronic compilation on the current state of studies in Europe is the *European Journal of American Studies* (*EJAS*). Marc Chénetier, the editor of this "flexible" and easily accessible collection of essays, writes in the "Introduction" of the 2006 inaugural issue that the journal is conceived as a new tool in "the hands of European Americanists" with which they "formulate and define their specific approach to the study of the United States" (2006). The primary aim of the *EJAS* was to survey "the potential new dimension" (2006) of the discipline across Europe in the twenty-first century, as presented by the members of the European Association for American Studies (EAAS) themselves. The first online issue published in 2006 featured the writings of members from Austria, Belarus, the Czech Republic, Slovakia, Finland, France, Germany, Greece, Hungary, Italy, Portugal, Romania, Russia, Spain, Switzerland, Turkey and the United Kingdom. Despite the abrasive criticism that appeared from its first issue—see Richard Ellis's article in which he conceives the journal as "fundamentally misconceived," "even retrograde" survey of "USAmerican studies" in Europe (14)—this journal definitely merits credit for being an open access, extensive e-compilation about the post-Cold War state of the discipline in Europe. Nevertheless, this pioneering enterprise edited by Chénetier, then the President of the European Association of American Studies then, was welcomed by most European practitioners of the field because it charted the situation of the discipline and its institutionalization at local, regional and national level with special regard to the discipline in our post-communist countries and brought into discussion germane questions, current problems and applicable methods in doing American studies in the current globalized world. The articles from the *EJAS* evince that American studies in Europe shares common features with what Kerber saw as the discipline's general state of "crisis" (419), the result of multiple strategies of its re-definition in various interdisciplinary domains within shifting political and academic discourses.

When talking about American studies, one has to be aware of the problems involved in the name of the discipline, as Janice Radway warned (1-32), and follow the developments in the methods, theories and institutions that perennially shape it. As the examples from *EJAS* show, our local, regional and national American studies reflect in a complex manner the ways in which this discipline positions and institutionalizes itself through diverse professional associations, through structure and content of the academic curricula, in pertinent publications (books, reviews, and journals), social networking websites and blogs, to name just a few.

Furthermore, all presidential addresses of the American Studies Association in the last two decades reflect on changes, transformations, critical issues and possible roads to be taken in mapping and practicing the discipline at a crossroads. In 1997, Patricia Nelson Limerick scrutinized the perimeters of the discipline when she delineated the research area of scholars researching the American West and observed that these researchers "have no borders, no limits, no division, by subject matter, of insiders and outsiders," except for the fact that they are brought together by their "shared interest in this very arbitrarily defined region, the American West" (455). The same was valid for the more general field of American studies. According to one of the best definitions so far, Limerick located this field as "the place of refuge for those who cannot find a home in the more conventional neighborhoods" and emphasized the importance of marginal discourses by describing the field as a "sanctuary for displaced hearts and minds, the place where no one is fully at ease" (452). In other words, American studies is as an interdisciplinary branch of knowledge that celebrates alterity in a cross-regional and transnational way. To describe this complex approach more accurately, Limerick introduced an intricate term for the American studies lexicon: she opted for a vernacular expression that went along with the construction, representation and production of a hybrid, transnational field she called "a heck of a thing" (457).

This "heck of a thing" marks the road now taken by most practitioners of American studies and unveils the multitude of questions inherent in the existing paradigms that operate within. To work with this "heck of a thing" means to be able to locate both "the heck" and "the thing" in the environment of our departments, institutes, universities and institutions by practicing new things as part of de-centered discourses of freedom fuelled by individual involvement in specific research topics and areas that are concerned with what many still try to define. Though seemingly unproblematic, it was not an easy task, for example, to define "the thing" and "the heck" of our own academic program when we put together a brief description for the website of the Department of American Studies at the University of Szeged having to use a number of far too general terms. We finally agreed that we would advertise "the thing" as a pool of studies focusing on "various aspects of American history, society (such as racial, ethnic, and religious groups, as well as women) and culture (including literature, film and the arts)" we approach "from a number of perspectives" when working with a "multiplicity of topics and methodological approaches" in order to "acquire analytical models" our students "can apply in examining other cultures and societies" with the "heck" of the "thing" laying in our added value emerging from the dialogic approaches to what America means here and now for us.

Moreover, we can widen our dialogic possibilities through the digital realm. In this context, it is our responsibility to work with new media and to take the new, digital 'roads' through which the locally nuanced human agency and its institutional context can be best 'linked' with the transnational spaces invoked and contained by the global field of American studies. American studies in Hungary is a young discipline adhering to the dynamic process of cultural and technological dissemination that seems to thrive inside and outside the classroom and does not even think of asking, as the nagging character of Donkey in *Shrek*: "[A]re we there yet?" (2001, dir. A. Adamson and V. Jenson). Wherever "there" is, we have already taken this digital road assuming that New American studies will be indeed new and challenging as long as there are practitioners who, as Chénetier writes, "do not feel compelled to follow the most-traveled roads" (2008).

***

Cultural Vistas and Sites of Identity. Essays on Literature, Film and American Studies is an enterprise on the route of New American studies employing among other most traveled roads, transnational American studies 2.0. This volume is the second publication and the first English language e-book of *AMERICANA eBook* series—a division of *AMERICANA E-Journal of American Studies in Hungary*, published by the Department of American Studies, University of Szeged, Hungary—which was established to promote the use of new media in our current practice of American studies. This open access e-book is part of a larger *AMERICANA* digital publishing project, which adopted new media practice and aims to become part of the current transnational dialogue in the field of New American studies.

Cultural Vistas and Sites of Identity. Essays on Literature, Film and American Studies is built around the complex issue of contemporary identity construction. Here, I reflect, similar to Kerber's subjective approach, on the representation of several American identities assembled in a heterogeneous compilation of essays concentrating on various American cultural vistas based on topics and texts I taught over the past years at my literature and film courses at the University of Szeged, Hungary. My aim was to (re)examine facets of various contemporary identity forms through a selection of American literary works (poems and dramas), alongside a number of films produced in the United States that present a challenge to diverse intradiegetic and extradiegetic identities. The context of New American studies provided a legitimate framework not only in the case of literary vistas but was crucial also for the context of film, itself an inherently transnational medium.

The present volume is divided into two distinct parts. The first, entitled "Sites of Identity Through Literary Vistas," examines the ways in which identity is constructed in the combined poetic works of two Latina writers, Aurora Levins Morales and her mother, Rosario Morales from *Getting Home Alive*, and in the controversial dramas of two queer authors, *The Goat of Who is Sylvia?* by Edward Albee and *How I Learnt to Drive* by Paula Vogel. The second part of the e-book, "Sites of Identity Through Cinematic Vistas" focuses on the representation of extradiegetic identity in films by discussing in the "Adaptation, Auteurship, and Identity" section the issues of identity as movie authorship in two film versions of *The Roman Spring of Mrs. Stone* by Tennessee Williams and in Mike Nichol's adaptation of Edward Albee's *Who's Afraid of Virginia Woolf?*. The last section, "Negotiation, Characters, and Identity," concentrates on the negotiations of intradiegetic identities in *Frida*, directed by Julie Taymor, and in the transnational context in Alejandro González Iñárritu's film, *Babel*.

Works Cited

Abádi-Nagy, Zoltán. (1995). "Editorial Note." *Hungarian Journal of English and American Studies*. 1.1. Web. Retrieved from: http://dragon.unideb.hu /~hjeas/history.html. Access: October 13, 2012.

---. (2009) "Anglisztika-amerikanisztika a mai Magyarországon." *Anglisztika és amerikanisztika. Magyar kutatások az ezredfordulón*. Eds. Frank Tibor and Károly Krisztina. Budapest: Tinta, 13-31. Print.

Adamson, Andrew and Vicky Jenson, dir. (2001). *Shrek*. Written by: William Steig, Screenplay: Ted Elliott, Terry Rossio, Joe Stillman, Roger S. H. Schulman, Music: Harry Gregson-Williams, John Powell, Cast: Mike Myers, Eddie Murphy,

Cameron Diaz, John Lithgrow. Distribution: DreamWorks Pictures through Universal Pictures Language: English, Runtime: 92 minutes. DVD.

Bollobás, Enikő. (2002). "Dangerous Liaisons: Politics and Epistemology in Post-Cold War American Studies." *American Quarterly*, 54. 4 (December): 563-579. Print.

Capucho, Maria Filomena. (2011). "Cooperating and Innovating—Redinter, Working Together for the Implementation of Intercomprehension Methodologies." *Proceedings of the June 16-17, 2011 Firenze International Conference "The Future of Education."* Web. Retrieved from: http://www.pixel-online.net/edu_future/common/download /Paper_pdf/ITL31-Capucho.pdf. Access: October 5, 2011.

Chénetier, Marc. (2006). "Introduction." *European Journal of American Studies*, 2006/1 *Varia*. Web. Retrieved from: http://ejas.revues.org /document528.html. Access: March 22, 2010.

---. (2008). " 'New' 'American Studies:' Exceptionalism redux?" *European Journal of American Studies*, 2008/2. Web. Retrieved from: http://ejas.revues.org/document7453.html. Access: April 3, 2010.

Cristian, Réka M. and Zoltán Dragon. (2005). "American Studies in the Age of Visual/Electronic Reproduction." *AMERICANA E-Journal of American Studies in Hungary*. Vol. 1, No.1. Fall. Web. Retrieved from: http://primus.arts.u-szeged.hu/american/americana/volIno1 /crmdz.htm. Access: March 26, 2010.

Dixon Gottschild, Brenda. (1999). "At the Crossroads: The American Studies/Performance Studies Intersection." From "Roundtable: The Imagined Community of International American Studies." *American Studies International*, XXXVIII/2 (June): 7-10. Print.

Elliott, Emory. (2007). "Diversity in the United States and Abroad: What Does It Mean When American Studies in Transnational?" *American Quarterly*, 59. 1 (March): 1-25. Print.

Ellis, Richard. (2006). "USAmerican Studies in the United Kingdom." *European Journal of American Studies*, 2006/1 *Varia*. Web. Retrieved from: http://ejas.revues.org/document448.html. Access: March 28, 2010.

Elteren, Mel van. (2006). "Rethinking Americanization Abroad: Toward a Critical Alternative to Prevailing Paradigms." *The Journal of American Culture*, 29. 3: 345-367. Print.

Farrell, James. J. (1999). "What Are American Studies For? Some Practical Perspectives." *American Studies*. 40. 2 (Summer): 183-197. Print.

Fishkin, Shelley Fisher. (2005). "Crossroads of Cultures: The Transnational Turn in American Studies. Presidential Address to the American Studies Association, November 12, 2004." *American Quarterly*, 57. 1 (March): 17-57. Print.

---. (2011). "Redefinitions of Citizenship and Revisions of Cosmopolitanism—Transnational Perspectives: A Response and a Proposal." *Journal of Transnational American Studies*, 3(1). Web. Retrieved from: http://escholarship.org/uc/item/1qw5364p. Access: August 29, 2011.

Giles, P. and R. J. Ellis. (2005). "E Pluribus Multitudinum: The New World of Journal Publishing in American Studies." *American Quarterly*, 57. 4 (December): 1033-1078. Print.

"Hacking the Academy. A Book Crowdsourced in One Week May 21-28, 2010," (2010). Web. Retrieved from: http://hackingtheacademy.org/. Access: August 16, 2011.

Howard, Alan B. (1999). "American Studies and the New Technologies." Web. Retrieved from: http://xroads.virginia.edu/~AS@UVA/SAAS/madrid.html. Access: March 31, 2010.

Kerber, Linda K. (1989). "Diversity and Transformation of American Studies." *American Quarterly*. 41. 3 (September): 415-431. Print.

Limerick, Patricia Nelson. (1997). "Insiders and Outsiders: The Borders of the USA and the Limits of the ASA: Presidential Address to the American Studies Association, 31 October 1996." *American Quarterly*, 49. 3 (September): 449-69. Print.

Montgomery, Maureen. (1999). "Introduction: The Construction of an international American Studies Community." From "Roundtable: The Imagined Community of International American Studies." *American Studies International*, XXXVIII/2 (June): 4-7. Print.

Oppermann, Matthias. (2010). "The World Wide Web and Digital Culture: New Borders, New Media, New American Studies." *A Concise Companion to American Studies*, Ed. John Carlos Rowe. Malden, Mass.: Wiley-Blackwell, 334-349. Print.

Pease, Donald. (2010). "Postnational and Postcolonial Reconfigurations of American Studies in the Postmodern Condition." *A Concise Companion to American Studies*, Ed. John Carlos Rowe. Malden, Mass.: Wiley-Blackwell, 263-283. Print.

Pultar, Gönül (1999). "The Imagined Community of American Studies in a Non-Christian, Non-'Western' Environment: American Studies Scholarship in Turkey." From "Roundtable: The Imagined Community of International American Studies," *American Studies International*. XXXVIII/2 (June): 11-14. Print.

Radway, Janice. (1999). "What's in a Name? Presidential Address to the American Studies Association, 20 November, 1998." *American Quarterly*, 51. 1 (March): 1-32. Print.

Rowe, John C. (2002). "Postnationalism, Globalism and the New American Studies." *The Futures of American Studies*. Eds. Donald E. Pease and Robyn Wiegman. Durham: Duke University Press, 167-182. Print.

Sato, Hiroko (1999). "The Rise and Relevance of American Studies in Japan." From "Roundtable: The Imagined Community of International American Studies," *American Studies International*, XXXVIII/2 (June): 14-17. Print.

Suiter, Tad. (2010). "Why 'Hacking'?," *Hacking the Academy. The Edited Volume*. Eds. Dan Cohen Dan and Tom Scheinfeldt. Ann Arbor: University of Michigan Press, digitalculturebooks. Web. Retrieved from: http://www.digitalculture.org/hacking-the-academy/introductions/#introductions-suiter. Access: August 16, 2011.

Sumida, Stephen H. (2003). "Where in the World Is American Studies? Presidential Address to the American Studies Association, Houston Texas, November 15, 2002." *American Quarterly*. 55. 3 (September): 333-351. Print.

Tucker, Bruce. (1999). "Canada in the Imagined Community of International American Studies." From "Roundtable: The Imagined Community of International American Studies." *American Studies International*. XXXVIII/2, (June): 17-23. Print.

CULTURAL VISTAS AND SITES OF IDENTITY

2. Sites of Identity Through Literary Vistas

The first part of the book is an incursion into the literary vistas of poems and dramas with special regard to the construction of contemporary American identities and is divided into two essays: "Border Stories and Posthegemonic Identities. Reading *Getting Home Alive*" and "Identities at Thresholds in *How I Learned to Drive* and *The Goat or Who Is Sylvia?*"

The first essay analyzes the post-nationalist identity construction in *Getting Home Alive* authored by Rosario Morales and her daughter, Aurora Levins Morales, who write their poems from a posthegemonic Americanist perspective. Their individual pieces, as well as their collaborative works, are samples of transgressive "border stories," providing critical insights into various facets of the *mestiza* identity made visible through issues of language, gender, race, and generations, all placed among the values and contradictions inherent in a variety of aspects of American life and culture.

The second text exposes and explores the identity crisis of the protagonists in Paula Vogel's *How I Learned to Drive* and Edward Albee's *The Goat or Who Is Sylvia?*, two dramas about taboos crafted into controversial allegories of incest and bestiality. Vogel and Albee address the question of marginalized identity in liminal situations by illuminating the thresholds their characters inhabit and the way in which they transgress the spaces of curious encounters.

2. 1. Border Stories and Posthegemonic Identities. Reading *Getting Home Alive*

AmeRícan, across forth and across back
back across and forth back
forth across and back and forth
our trips are walking bridges!
Tato Laviera

To survive in the Borderlands
you must live *sin fronteras*
be a crossroads.
Gloria Anzaldúa

In her analysis of life narratives, interdisciplinarity and post-nationalism, Barbara Brinson Curiel claims that "[We] are surrounded by border-crossings of the real and the metaphorical variety" (201). Indeed, we encounter a multitude of situations involving real or abstract borders in many aspects of life and culture. The concept of the border for Curiel is a powerful metaphor, the basic trope in the discussion of political, racial, and social borderlands (202) present in many autobiographies, biographies, ethnographic narratives, music, and in various forms of fiction. According to Gloria Anzaldúa, a border is "set up to define the places that are safe and unsafe" (25), denoting "a dividing line, a narrow strip along a steep edge" (25) that generally defines the geographical and political perimeters of two or more neighboring states. However, borderland mentality goes beyond imposed borders, including the "vague and undetermined place created by the emotional residue of an unnatural boundary" that is can sometimes be a no man's land "in a constant state of transition" (25). Borderlands for Anzaldúa are thus real and mental zones wherein the "prohibited" and the "forbidden" exist in a turbulent ambiance, a site of transgression for *los atravesados* (25) that cross over limit and traverse zones passing through constricted areas of control and subterfuge.

The aim of this chapter is to investigate the construction of identity in this vague and ambivalent region of the borderlands in the works of Rosario Morales and her daughter, Aurora Levins Morales. They published *Getting Home Alive* in 1986, a book that contains both the individual and collaborative pieces—poetry and short prose—of Morales and Levins Morales. Their literary team-work represents a segment of American minority literature not only in terms of gender but also in terms of ethnicity because both authors depict the crossing of various borders when they write about the issue of language, generations, gender, and race by embracing both a postcolonial stance and a post-national attitude to culture in general.

The posthegemonic perspective, as Donald Pease and Robyn Wiegman write, is a subcategory of the post-national American studies approach, emerged as an "open-ended circuit of transnational and international relations as a strategic substitution for nationalism" (26). Both posthegemonic and counterhegemonic attitudes derive from the discourses that various social movement "produce as they traverse and intersect with disciplinary formations" (27). The writers of *Getting Home Alive* subscribe to a posthegemonic strategy rather than to a counterhegemonic approach and construct their identity accordingly. The posthegemonic elements are represented in the book of the mother and the daughter through a radical cultural pluralization that redefines difference by continuous reshaping of the mainstream and the margins within an ever evolving paradigm of newness.

As a result of the ongoing processes of literary recanonization, Levins Morales is currently included in some anthologies of American Literature. The second edition of *The Heath Anthology of American Literature* (Vol. Two), for example, contains her poems and a short piece in the chapter "*New* Communities, *New* Identities, and *New* Energies" (2389). According to this classification, Levins Morales is ranked "new" due to the difference in identity politics her work offers. Interestingly, the fifth edition of the same anthology published twelve years later has a revised criteria of categorization and enlists Levins Morales in the more general cluster of "New Generations: Postmodernity and Difference" (2345), which envelops a more inclusive designation of her works at the beginning of the third millennium. This inclusion indicates a posthegemonic shift in attitude regarding the placement of other similar authors and suggests a parallel strategy for the interpretation of her texts. On a more general level, this categorization seems to be in tandem with the new directions of posthegemonic, New American studies, as Pease and Wiegman claim, "emerge out of the reinstituting powers that social movements produce as they traverse and intersect with disciplinary formations" (27) resulting in interdisciplinary cultural crossroads products, such as the works of Morales and Levins Morales.

For these two women, American identity means being simultaneously ethnic or 'different' and hybrid or 'new.' At this point, newness and difference can be considered constitutive features of a complex identity; their writings, accordingly, depict novel and distinct facets of identity by crossing genres (poetry and prose) and dual authors (Rosario Morales and Aurora Levins Morales). Their texts themselves are, to use Curiel's term, "border stories" providing critical insights into the values and contradictions inherent in a variety of aspects of American life and culture.

In the following, the analysis will be based on a selection of poems and prose from *Getting Home Alive* with special focus on "Child of the Americas" written by Levins Morales and on the "Ending Poem," signed by both authors. *Getting Home Alive* incorporates real and metaphorical border situations and various types of boundary crossings. The short *belles-lettres* pieces included in this book are not only descriptive sites but also they are, to use Carole Boyce Davies's words, critical standpoints revealing "cross-cultural, transnational, translocal, diasporic perspectives" (996) that classify them as postcolonial texts interwoven into the American context.

The poems and short pieces of *Getting Home Alive* are the result of a dialogic process between its writers but also express a dialogic vision about the world they live in. The dialogic relation—as defined by Mikhail Bakhtin—is a concept encapsulating for example, the perennial dialogue of a work of art with other works of art, of an author with other authors (57, 59) and stands at the basis of virtually all intertextual connections. In *Getting Home Alive* this dialogic mother-daughter relation of mutual influence is emphasized in the two "Introduction/Acknowledgments" parts that reveal the birth of the book as a common enterprise. Rosario Morales (the creator of the book's cover art) explains her share of dialogism in creating the pieces of the volume with the maternal metaphors of nurturing and umbilical cord:

> This book began in long budget-braking telephone calls stretched across the width of this country, in "listen to what I've just written;" in "did you hear about this book, this song, this poem, this event?" It began because Rosario wrote rhymes at eleven and not again until she was in her forties and Aurora wrote poetic thoughts when she was seven and was a working writer and teacher when her mother started up again, each influencing the other willy-nilly, through the good times and the bad, the fights and the making up, the long sullen silences and the happy chatter cluttering the phone line strung between us like a 3000-mile umbilical cord from navel to navel, mine to hers, hers to mine, each of us mother and daughter by turns, feeding each other the substance of our dreams. ("Introduction/Acknowledgments," Cambridge, MA, May 1986)

Her daughter, Aurora Levins Morales, describes this dialogic creative process emphasizing the continuous process of mutual teaching, even through the periods when she was silent. She writes that

> [A]t some point, interwoven with our book reviews, we began to read each other our writing as well. "I have a new piece... whaddya think?" [...] Like other mothers and daughters we have our yelling matches, the anger and silences between us. But we have always had this, too: that we are teachers to each other, that we love the power of our own and each other's lives, that we are able to see beyond the mother-daughter knot to where the bond is. [...] There, we join forces to think about the world, about women's lives, and about how being who we are has shaped us. There, we send each other postcards of women writing, write about each other's lives, read each other1s work to audiences and friends. This book is the blossoming of that cross-fertilization. My mother taught me how to read. Together, we have taught ourselves to be writers. ("Introduction/Acknowledgments," Oakland, CA, May 1986)

Another important dialogical connection between the works and authors pertaining to this volume is Gloria Anzaldúa's *Borderlands/La Frontera* (1987), published a year after the collection of poems and personal essays of *Getting Home Alive* was released. The motto poem on page 14 of *Getting Home Alive* is an excerpt from Anzaldúa's *Borderlands*, then a work in progress. This reference, specified as a curious metadata on the editorial page of *Getting Home Alive*, was taken from the "forthcoming book by the same name [*Borderlands*] to be published by Spinster-Aunt Lute." This uncommon reference acknowledges Anzaldúa's work as significant intertextual influence and is proof of the collaboration among these three authors. Anzaldúa's theoretical text informs and heralds thus a special type of postcolonial literature about borderlands as exemplified by Morales and Levins Morales.

As Ania Loomba claims, the term "postcolonial" has recently become "heterogeneous and diffuse" (xii) because of its interdisciplinary nature. Even its spelling varies: depending on the discipline, the term appears hyphenated (used mostly in reference to the historical period after colonization) and non-hyphenated (referring mostly to the theoretical context), with a concomitant shifting of the concept's definition. Since Postcolonial Studies are connected in many regards with Ethnic Studies, there is a growing academic awareness in the U.S. and worldwide about the overlapping of former with latter. In the introduction to the chapter on "Ethnic Studies, Post-Coloniality, and International Studies" Julie Rivkin and Michael Ryan observed that the "thinkers in the field of post-colonial studies tend to be more skeptical of ethnic identity than Post-Structuralist philosophers outside the field" (855) and opt for a less parochial view. Ethnic Studies has a quite restrictive character—similar to the discourse of colonialism—by reinforcing, as Curiel states, "the counterproductive idea that whites and the middle class have no culture, and that only some ('other') groups of people have noteworthy social and cultural experiences" ("Migratory Subjectivities" 216). Under these circumstances, post-national and posthegemonic American studies incorporate, as the group of authors of the "Introduction" to *Post-Nationalist American Studies* volume write, underlying postcolonial strategies by adopting a critical practice of promoting a less insular and a "more internationalist and comparative" (2) view on specific cultural issues. In this sense, the post-national, posthegemonic method reflects the "negotiation among local, national, and global frames of analysis that seek its justification neither in objective and progressive historical processes of globalization nor in implicit celebrations of the obliteration of the local and national" (8). In the following, I will apply the 'postcolonial' term to the specificities of American culture instead of 'ethnic' in the description of identity construction. The latter, especially when referring to ethnic identity, creates numerous ideological limitations, whereas postcolonial identity bears a more complex connotation in describing cultural discourses of the United States and provides a step forward in understanding the construction of the posthegemonic American identity. As Barbara Brinson Curiel, David Kazanjian, Katherine Kinney, Steven Mailloux, Jay Mechling, John Carlos Rowe, George Sánchez, Shelley Streeby, Henry Yu claim, Postcolonial Studies together with critical internationalism play a crucial role in the contemporary cultural practices in the United States today (7), providing the most challenging approaches on issues of (trans)nation(al), race, language, and gender. Feminism and Postcolonial Studies have revived the name of the author from its poststructuralist hibernation: in a postcolonial reading of a text the author becomes a source of further meanings with possible connotations. In this case—to paraphrase Anzaldúa—what validates one as a human being, validates one as writer, too.

For example, recent American literary anthologies present a biographical bird's eye view about the life of the writer before the actual literary text; therefore, fiction and non-fiction border each other under a heading that provides a number of works and also references about the author's life and the reception of her or his works. For Curiel, the boundary between fiction and non-fiction is assembled here in the process of transgressing generic borders (204). In the posthegemonic approach—as I wrote in "Telling Woman"—, there is no 'objective' narrative but many 'subjective' decentered stories and plots "scattered and grounded in specific cultural-political realms" (46) which provide the pillars for identity construction. In Kathleen Stewart's words, these stories, written from the margins be they ethnic, racial or gender ones are "spaces on the side of the road" that help define subjects by also (re)defining the "road" itself (7) that used to be paved with what Anzaldúa saw as dominant, unquestionable, and unchallengeable paradigms (38). Morales and Levins Morales wrote texts that can be read and interpreted as posthegemonic "border stories" and as literary "spaces on the side of the road" that reevaluate existing paradigms.

Aurora Levins Morales (born 1954 in Indiera, Puerto Rico) is an American poet-activist who was influenced from early childhood by her mother's love of literature. Rosario Morales (born in 1930 in Puerto Rico) and her daughter have both Jewish and Puerto Rican mixed ancestry. The works of Levins Morales focus on the cultural cross-fertilization among Northern Anglo-American, Latin American and Caribbean cultures. She considers herself a "mixed heritage person" because she has "grown up in coalitions" that make her identify primarily "with Latin American writers, female and male" ("Testimonies to Survival" 1995). Nevertheless, the influence on her writing were mostly "U.S. women of color" that provided her main "literary home base" ("Testimonies to Survival" 1995). According to Frances R. Aparicio, Levins Morales defines her *mestiza* and "female identity through an analysis and critique" (3026) of the two cultures she inhabits: Puerto Rican and U.S. American. As a genuine *mestiza*, she is, in Anzaldúa's context, the "product of the transfer of the cultural and spiritual values of one group to another" facing the dilemma of the mixed breed" in the struggle of various borders (100) she writes about.

Generally, border stories reconceptualize a variety of cultural frameworks as they construct identities at the crossroads of the Americas. By citing the works of José Saldívar and Vicente Diaz about the complexities of borderland culture, Janice Radway suggested that

> identity must be conceptualized as a specific, always changing relationship to multiple, shifting, imagined communities, communities which, despite the fact that they are always imagined, are situated in specific places at particular moments and amidst particular geographies. (15)

"Child of the Americas" is a powerful example of such literary identity construction. From the first line of the poem, Levins Morales uses a specific, confessional language by placing a peculiar stylistic and linguistic competence at the core of identity construction. The lyrical "I," written in first person singular, suggests an intimate aesthetic distance from autobiographical data. Additionally, this "I" of the poem resonates a complex ethnic mixture into a polyphonic construction: the voice of a "light skinned mestiza of the Caribbean" mingled with that of a "U.S. Puerto Rican Jew," product of "the ghettos of New York I have never known" that communicates her gendered, racial and religious identity in a specific English, which is "the tongue of [her] consciousness" while Spanish is in her "flesh" (50). She is proud of her immigrant ancestry by emphasizing that she is "[a]n immigrant and the daughter and granddaughter of immigrants," shortly, "a child of many diaspora" (50) in a seemingly borderless world.

Speaking from the edges of the continent and from the margins of the mainstream culture, Morales uses geographical tropes in defining her identity as "Caribeña." For Anthony Appiah, the Caribbean region's "politico-linguistic geography" (950) is one of the main sites of identity production showing pertinent images reflecting what Morales calls the "idiosyncracies of her nature" ("Puertoricanness" 85). In the renewed geography of "Child of the Americas" the Caribbean is a region of multiplicity, an archipelago at ideological, cultural, political and geographical crossroads, a complex vista of mixed ancestry. The lyrical voice speaks English, the tongue of her consciousness, "with passion" and Spanish, "the languages of garlic and mangoes" embodied in her "flesh" (50). Because her "first language was spanglish" (50), there is no hierarchy between English and Spanish; these two languages are equal components of a subjective tongue born at the geopolitical and linguistic crossroads.

In this poem, the *mestiza* connotes more than a cultural hybrid person; in Breyten Breytenbach's view, a *mestizo/a* practices "nomadic thinking" and is a "transient and mutating" character with a "vivid consciousness of being the Other" (57). This "transient" person belongs to the "Middle World" by recognizing affinities with similar people from the community of "Global Village vagrants" (47, 58). For Morales, identity is expressed by multiple origins resulting in the affirmation of what she is but also in the negation of a number of ancestral imagined communities. Walking along an imaginary line of the material world, she is similar to the subjects of Lila Downs's songs from the album entitled *La Línea* (2001) who are transgressing imaginary and real boundaries.

Identity in "The Child of the Americas" reflects a Breytenbachian "number of negative affinities" (57) in relation with the places of origin and cultural roots. Moreover, the elimination of capital letters in this poem emphasizes a posthegemonic approach to any hierarchical of one place over another. As such, African ancestry appears as a reflection of the continent and devolves into the newly conceived word, "african;" the native Caribbean Taino lineage becomes the gendered, distant "taina" while Europe fades into the attenuated "european" form.

> I am not african. Africa is in me, but I cannot return.
> I am not taina. Taino is in me, but there is no way back.
> I am not european. Europe lives in me, but I have no home there.
> (50)

As "child of the Americas," the subject of the poem lives in an in-between space, in what Anzaldúa coined as *los intersticios*, in the space be-tween worlds, a Middle World type of space defined by Anzaldúa as "life in the borderlands" (42). Unlike Anzaldúa's spineless "nopal de castilla" (67), the lyrical "I" of this poem is far from being a defenseless cactus. Over-coming the tradition of silence she gains a powerful voice, more effective than the spines of any desert plant. "I am new. / History made me. My first language was spanglish. / I was born at the crossroads / and I am whole" (50), Morales writes (50). As the "new" offspring of Americas, "born into this continent at a crossroads," she assigns this borderland space as her site of origin and voice. She defines a version of American identity, where "newness" is ambiguous in terms of ethnicity, nationality and citizen-ship and also devoid of any hegemony. Besides, the "child" metaphor in "child of Americas" alludes to new beginnings and visions reconciling un-der the plural concept of "Americas," an intricate coexistence recalling José Martí's "Our America."

An expanded version of "Child of the Americas," the "Ending Poem" is a lyrical elaboration of the posthegemonic approach. This poem has two authors: the mother, Rosario, and the daughter, Aurora, and is a reconfigu-ration of "Child of the Americas" in a unique combination of mother and daughter written in two distinct voices. While in "The Child of the Ameri-cas" the singular voice of "I" inhabited a plural continent, "Ending Poem," set as the last work of *Getting Home Alive* volume, starts speaking in the sin-gular and ends in the plural "we" about the same "Americas" site. The dis-tinction between voices is achieved by bold letters alternating with normal typography in the layout of the poem. "I am what I am" is the first line re-calling Rosario Morales's identity poem with the same title. In this short confessional, Rosario defines herself by the cultures of displacement she has encountered. Besides being "U.S. American" and "Puerto Rican," among many other identity markers, she considers herself part of the place she lives in and which, in turn, shapes her identity:

> I am what I am and I am U.S. American [...] I am Puerto Rican [...]
> I am new York Manhattan and the Bronx [...] I am what I am I am
> Boricua as Boricuas come from the isle of Manhattan [...] I am what
> I am and I'm naturalized Jewish-American" ("I Am What I Am"
> 138-139)

The ongoing process of self-reconfiguration in the "Ending Poem" reaches, besides the alternating typography of interchanging voices, bilin-gual dimensions in the use of English and Spanish words. The "child of many diasporas" ("Ending Poem" 212) is also the "child of many mothers" (213) that appears as a "mountain-born, country-bred, homegrown jíbara child/ *up from the shtetl, a California Puerto Rican Jew*" who does not know the names of the ancestors but "*[F]irst names only, or mija, negra, ne, honey, sugar, dear*" (212). The blend of multiple cultural backgrounds, the *mestizaje*, is symbolized in the poem by a table cloth "woven by one, dyed by another, / *embroidered by another still*" (213) and which appears also in a picture on the cover of the book as the artwork of Rosario Morales. The closing lines of the "Ending Poem" rewrite the last lines of "Child of the Americas" in a plural blending:

> We are new.
> *They gave us life, kept us going.*
> brought us to where we are
> *Born at the crossroads.* (213)

"Ending Poem" inherited many features from previous pieces written by Rosario Morales, and especially from the rhetoric of identity found in "I Am the Reasonable One," a short prose about the inner struggle of the woman striving to survive in a complex world of words and things where "self-expression is so limited by your self-repression" ("I Am the Reasonable One" 147). A reasonable container of unsaid tensions, the owner of the narrative voice ceases to be "reasonable" and decides to become angry by raising her voice and consciousness. She adopts a counterhegemonic discourse of anger and revolt; she will not "eat herself up inside anymore" (149). Instead, the lyrical "I" adopts a radical tone and is ready to fight the outside world by saying that "I am going to eat you" (149). These lines, echoed in the "Ending Poem" in an attenuated form, show that the counterhegemonic attitude of the mother's discourse shifted to a posthegemonic position in the poem of the mother and daughter. The devouring woman is transformed in "Ending Poem" into a mother figure who feeds her children at a table decorated with a symbolic, *mestizo/a* dishcloth. The transformation appears after the line "I am a child of many mothers" ("Ending Poem" 213), where the "I" turns plural in a historical perspective:

> They have kept it all going
> All the civilizations erected on their backs.
> All the dinner parties given with their labor" (213).

"We" is the collective pronoun for "their" children with whom now, having a voice, "they" talk directly. "Eat, dear, eat," these mothers say, and unlike angry parents swallowing up the addressee, they nurture "us" with words.

> Come, lay that dishcloth down. Eat, dear, eat.
> *History made us.*

We will not eat ourselves up inside anymore.
And we are whole. (213)

"Child of the Americas" and "Ending Poem" are intertextual transgressions reflecting (on) the writers' identity quest within the postcolonial context. They are, as Günter Lenz observed, dialogic texts in the "vein of the Bakhtinian notions of dialogism, heteroglossia, and hybridization, of the intertextual relations between discourses" and present an "internal dialogization and differentiation of discourses in their specific historical and social contexts" (474). Aurora Levins Morales and Rosario Morales combine languages, cultures and places to portray a *mestiza* identity constructed in the cultural borderlands. The(ir) life in the cultural borderlands involves an Anzaldúan intimate linguistic terrorism (42), one that overcomes the "tradition of silence" (76). This linguistic transgression is conditioned by a nomadic cultural identity that appears at the border of two (or more) languages and cultures and reflects crossings over the boundary between silence and utterance, as well as that between two languages in acts of literary hybridization. In "Borderlands/La Frontera: The New Mestiza" Anzaldúa calls this type of language *el lenguaje de la frontera*, the language of the border.

Levins Morales employs a similar border language when she writes about a Puerto Rican woman living in north Oakland in her short prose "Puertoricanness." This woman 'imports' Caribbean Latino culture with the words, with plants and food, with the sounds and the culinary taste of her native land and mingles it into a functional border language that fuses Spanish and English into a hybrid "exchange" that finally becomes a variant of vernacular American English when she speaks about her daily experience:

> Since she could not right now, in the endless bartering of a woman with two countries., bring herself to trade in one-half of her heart for the other, exchange this loneliness for another perhaps harsher one, she would live as Puerto Rican lives en la isla [on the island], right here in north Oakland, plant the bananales [banana plants] and cafetales [coffee trees] of her heart around her bedroom door, sleep under the shadow of their bloom and the carving hoarseness of the roosters, wake to the blue-rimmed white enamel cups of jugo de piña [pineapple juice] and plates of guineo verde [green bananas or Plaintains], and heat pots of rice with bits of meat in them on the stove all day. (85-86)

As a Puerto Rican, "she" inhabits what Appiah calls a "Western architecture" (953) both in terms of language (English) and of location (Oakland). This linguistic register imposes a special syntax on the written text but proves insufficient for Caribbean words in Spanish that are frequently inserted in the bilingual sentences. To enhance a better understanding of the text, *The Heath Anthology of American Literature* (both the older and the newer version) provide these words with translated footnotes. The spirit of "Puertoricanness" here shows similar features to that of the "two-ness" of African-Americans described by William Edward Burghardt Du Bois in "The Souls of Black Folk" (1903) in which African Americans have "two souls, two thoughts, two unreconciled strivings; two warring ideals in one dark body, whose dogged strength alone keeps it from being torn asunder" (898). In "Puertoricanness," this "two-ness" becomes a more complicated construction, involving gender, religion, and language in the identity profile of the Puerto Rican voice.

The elements combining the identity of the Puerto Rican woman in the U.S. appear in this short Latina *écriture féminine* as the Caribbean "soup of signs" one has to combine linguistically and culturally in order to understand the essence of a possible postcolonial identity that Antonio Benítez-Rojo calls the "union of the diverse" (979). Rosario Morales's and Aurora Levins Morales's portrayal of identity resembles "a cultural meta-archipelago without center and without limits" that presents the person of the lyrical "I" metaphorically as a "repeating island," one that "proliferates endlessly" (985) when it comes to define identity in terms of linguistic, racial or gender borders. Morales and Levins Morales are in essence postcolonial and American writers, and authors also of the Middle World writing, across generations, with a posthegemonic attitude. For Levins Morales, "Caribeña" and "Puertorican" means an individual who has been "born" at the "crossroads" and who had been made "whole;" for Morales "puertorican" (148) is a state of things, an integral condition that must be lived. This integrity exists because the subject which it refers to is not the product of a single homogenous culture, but is the result of multiple fertilization, a bastardization of cultures through which she becomes a "child of the Americas." America is a plural place, while "Americas" embodies a virtual site with no generic borders that overcomes any geographical categorization, and covers the issue of plural, posthegemonic identity.

In her article on border stories, Curiel writes about the migration of the Latino population describing the legal and illegal border-crossings of the Mexicans to the U.S. She discovers—similar to Rosairo Morales and Aurora Levins Morales—that, after the actual act of crossing the border, in the process of shaping a mixed identity, one needs to consider the implied elements of cultural and linguistic transgressions (201). Similarly, Levins Morales shapes her identity with the terms "new" and "whole," both born at the "crossroads" of Americas. Her lyrical "I" is a hybrid construction, the result of crossing cultural and linguistic borders. Since the definition of identity in this case is postcolonial by means of implied ethnicity and cultural transgression within the U.S., the term of posthegemonic American becomes a matter of postcolonial definition, too. Born within the political borders of the U.S., Rosario Morales and Aurora Levins Morales employ an inverse method of identity construction: they first detach themselves and each other from the 'outside,' region of the Caribbean, Africa and Europe and only then from the 'inside' U.S. For both mother and daughter, identity appears both as the crossroads product of a subjective border language and as a border story told in that tongue. Carefully avoiding the term 'American,' both writers prefer the notion of "I," "child of Americas," and "we" that reflects their posthegemonic perspective towards political borders and political markers of identity.

The syncretism of culturally complex Americas mirrored in the self-reflexive portrait of the lyrical and narratorial voices in the above-mentioned texts results in specific cultural border stories that reflect liminal spaces of encounter. These discursive zones recontextualize the sense of "new" identities because they are at the same time acts of post-national identity formation and processes that Homi K. Bhabha calls "cultural translation" (938). A postcolonial, cross-generational reading of contemporary Latina literary texts can create a special chiasmic interpretation that promotes an inherently creative dissent (rather than consensus) and alterity (rather than conformity) in the American literary canon and in the shaping of the post-national, posthegemonic American identity. This is the interpretive site of the Middle World, an interstitial site, where according to Bhabha, "non-consensual forms of affiliations" (941) occur and are established.

In defining the contested term "American" in the context of postcolonial readings performed on canonized American texts, one must be aware, as Bhabha shows, that the "concepts of homogenous national cultures, the consensual or contiguous transmission of historical traditions, or 'organic' ethnic communities—as the grounds of cultural comparativism—are in profound process of redefinition" (936), in which the categories of identity are made salient by special, dominant cultural codes. These categories of identity intersect, transfigure, and continually redefine each other—as the texts of Morales has shown—and can mark the very context they are placed in (canonization in anthologies and modes of interpretation).

Postcolonial theory has been keen to label individuals as 'ethnic' and to build theories of ethnicity on the basis of this label. Both Rosario Morales and Aurora Levins Morales exceed this ideological marker because their works present an "Americas" identity that transcends not only the boundaries of generations, languages and cultures but also the boundaries of the postcolonial theory, while being grounded in the same context. Nevertheless, postcolonial and post-national identities are not, as Lindon Barrett explains, mutually exclusive because "as much as ethnic/racial formations prove dissociative or diacritical, they are also profoundly syncretic" (305). And it is this Middle World syncretism present in the "Americas" that forms the basis of a dialogic understanding of contemporary American identities that helps readers understand New American studies from a posthegemonic perspective.

Works Cited

Anzaldúa, Gloria. (1999). *Borderlands/La Frontera*. San Francisco: Aunt Lute Books. Print.

Aparicio, Frances R. (2006) ."Aurora Levins Moralas." *The Heath Anthology of American Literature*. Vol. E. *Contemporary Period: 1945 to the Present*, Gen. ed. Paul Lauter. Boston: Houghton Mifflin Company, 3026-3027. Print.

Appiah, Anthony. (1998). "Topologies of Nativism." *Literary Theory: An Anthology*. Eds. Julie Rivkin and Michael Ryan. Malden, Mass.: Blackwell, 945-957. Print.

Bahtyin, Mihail. (2001). *Dosztojevszkij poétikájának problémái*. Trans. Csaba Könczöl, Katalin Szőke, István Hevesi, Géza Horváth, Budapest. Gond-Cura/Osiris. Print.

Barrett, Lindon. (2002). "Identity and Identity Studies: Reading Toni Cade Bambara's 'The Hammer Man.'" *The Futures of American Studies*. Eds. Donald E. Pease and Robyn Wiegman. Durham: Duke University Press, 305-326. Print.

Benítez-Rojo, Antonio. (1998). "The Repeating Island." *Literary Theory: An Anthology*. Eds. Julie Rivkin and Michael Ryan. Malden, Mass.: Blackwell, 978-995. Print.

Bhabha, Homi K. (1998). "The Location of Culture." *Literary Theory: An Anthology*. Eds. Julie Rivkin and Michael Ryan. Malden, Mass.: Blackwell, 936-944. Print.

Breytenbach, Breyten. (1999). "Notes from the Middle World." *The Translatability of Cultures. Proceedings of the Fifth Stuttgart Seminar in Cultural Studies 03.08-14.08.1998*. Ed. Heide Ziegler. Stuttgart: Metzler, 47-63. Print.

Cristian, Réka M. (2002)."Telling Woman: Historias Orales de Mujeres Húngaras." Trans. Servando Ortoll. *Estudios Sobre Las Culturas Contemporaneas. Programa Cultura: Revista de investigation y análisis*. Centro Universitario de Investigationes Sociales. Universidad de Colima. Mexico. Epoca II, VII/ 16 (Diciembre): 37-53. Print.

Curiel, Barbara Brinson. (2000). "My Border Stories: Life Narratives, Interdisciplinarity, and Post-Nationalism in Ethnic Studies." *Post-Nationalist American Studies*. Ed. John Carlos Rowe. Berkeley: California University Press, 200-218. Print.

Curiel, Barbara Brinson, David Kazanjian, Katherine Kinney, Steven Mailloux, Jay Mechling, John Carlos Rowe, George Sánchez, Shelley Streeby, Henry Yu. (2000). "Introduction." *Post-Nationalist American Studies*. Ed. John Carlos Rowe. Berkeley: California University Press, 1-21. Print.

Davies, Carole Boyce. (1998). "Migratory Subjectivities." *Literary Theory: An Anthology*. Eds. Julie Rivkin and Michael Ryan. Malden, Mass.: Blackwell, 996-1015. Print.

Doughty, Julia. (1995). "Testimonies to Survival: Notes from an interview with Aurora Levins Morales." *Standards. The International Journal of Multicultural Studies. Fifth Anniversary Issue. "Survival."* 5/1 (Fall). Web. Retrieved from:

http://www.colorado.edu/journals/standards/V5N1/essays/morales_int.html. Access: November 15, 2010.

Downs, Lila. (2001). *La Linea/Border.* Producers: Paul Cohen, Aneiro Tano, Lila Downs. Lila Downs (vocals, guiro); Ken Basman (electric guitar); Celso Duarte (guitar, violin, harp); Rodrigo Duarte (cello); Carlos "Poppis" Touar (ocarina, bongos, congas, guiro, percussion, background vocals); Paul Cohen (clarinet, tenor saxophone, keyboards); Alfredo Pino (trumpet); Gabriel Hernandez (piano); Aneiro Tano (Fender Rhodes piano); Agustin Bernal (acoustic bass); Omar Aran (drums); Carlos "Pelusa" Rivarola (cajon, djembe, percussion); Armando "Pinaca" Espinosa (percussion); Memo Diaz (background vocals). Recorded at Al Studios, Mexico City. CD.

Du Bois, W. E. B. (2006). "The Souls of Black Folk." *The Heath Anthology of American Literature, Volume D. Modern Period: 1910-1945.* Fifth Edition. Gen. ed. Paul Lauter. Boston: Houghton Mifflin Company, 897-917. Print.

Lauter, Paul, gen. ed. (1994). *The Heath Anthology of American Literature.* Second Edition. Vol. Two, Lexington, Mass.: D.C. Heath and Company. Print.

---. (2006). *The Heath Anthology of American Literature.* Vol. E. *Contemporary Period: 1945 to the Present,* Boston: Houghton Mifflin Company. Print.

Lenz, Günter H. (2002) "Toward a Dialogics of International American Culture Studies: Transntionality, Border Discourses, and Public Culture(s)." *The Futures of American Studies.* Eds. Donald E. Pease and Robyn Wiegman. Durham: Duke University Press, 461-485. Print.

Loomba, Ania. (1998). *Colonialism/Postcolonialism.* London: Routledge. Print.

Martí, José. (2006). "Our America." *The Heath Anthology of American Literature, Volume C. Late Nineteenth Century: 1865-1910.* Fifth Edition. Gen. ed. Paul Lauter. Boston: Houghton Mifflin Company, 831-838. Print.

Morales, Aurora Levins. (1986). "Child of the Americas." *Getting Home Alive.* Aurora Levins Morales and Rosario Morales. Ithaca, New York: Firebrand Books, 50. Print.

---. (1986). "Puertoricanness." *Getting Home Alive.* Aurora Levins Morales and Rosario Morales. Ithaca, New York: Firebrand Books, 84-86. Print.

Morales, Rosario. (1986). "I Am What I Am." *Getting Home Alive.* Aurora Levins Morales and Rosario Morales. Ithaca, New York: Firebrand Books, 138-139. Print.

---. (1986). "I Am the Reasonable One." *Getting Home Alive.* Aurora Levins Morales and Rosario Morales. Ithaca, New York: Firebrand Books, 147-149. Print.

Morales, Aurora Levins and Rosario Morales. (1986). "Ending Poem." *Getting Home Alive.* Aurora Levins Morales and Rosario Morales. Ithaca, New York: Firebrand Books, 212-213. Print.

Pease, Donald E. and Robyn Wiegman. (2002). "Futures." *The Futures of American Studies.* Eds. Pease, Donald E. and Robyn Wiegman. Durham: Duke University Press, 1-42. Print.

Radway, Janice. (1999). "What's in a Name? Presidential Address to the American Studies Association. 20 November 1998." *American Quarterly* 51.1 (March): 1-32. Print.

Rivkin, Julie and Ryan, Michael. (1998). "English Without Shadows, Literature on a World Scale." *Literary Theory: An Anthology*. Eds. Julie Rivkin and Michael Ryan. Malden, Mass.: Blackwell, 850-855. Print.

Rowe, John Carlos. (2002). "Postnationalism, Globalism, and the New American Studies." *The Futures of American Studies*. Eds. Donald E. Pease and Robyn Wiegman. Durham: Duke University Press, 167-182. Print.

Stewart, Kathleen. (1996). *A Space on the Side of the Road. Cultural Poetics in an "Other"America*. Princeton, Princeton University Press. Print.

2. 2. Identities at Thresholds in *How I Learned to Drive* and *The Goat or Who Is Sylvia?*

> An identity is questioned only when it is menaced, as when the mighty begin to
> fall, or when the wretched begin to rise, or when the stranger enters the gates,
> never, thereafter, to be a stranger. Identity would seem to be the garment with
> which one covers the nakedness of the self: in which case, it is best that the gar-
> ment be loose, a little like the robes of the desert, through which one's nakedness
> can always be felt, and, sometimes, discerned. This trust in one's nakedness is all
> that gives one the power to change one's robes.
>
> *James A. Baldwin*

This chapter will explore the thresholds of characters identity in Paula Vogel's *How I Learned to Drive* (1997) and Edward Albee's *The Goat or Who Is
Sylvia?* (2002). These dramas touch upon taboo subjects crafted into controversial allegories of incest and bestiality. One prestigious precursor of
these dramas of identity polemics was Tony Kushner's two-part work *Angels in America: A Gay Fantasia on National Themes. Part One: Millenium Approaches* (1991) and *Angels in America: A Gay Fantasia on National Themes. Part
Two: Perestroika* (1992) in which he created an image of the United States of
America where, according to C. W. E. Bigsby, "religious, racial, sexual identities co-exist and intermingle" in order to shape a world in which "the
breaching of boundaries is both method and subject" (*Modern American
Drama* 423). The transgression of boundaries in Kushner's play takes place
in the context of gender and political issues. He contextualizes and depicts
his characters within the *Zeitgeist* of the eighties and nineties—AIDS, political innuendos, race and homosexuality—which he dramatizes in an manner
comparable only to the dramatic world of Vogel's and Albee's plays.

The choices of dramatic genre and of *How I Learned to Drive* along with *The Goat or Who Is Sylvia?* were initially conditioned by the general marginalized position of dramas in the American literary canon. According to Susan Harris Smith, until the 1980s American drama was considered an "unwanted bastard child" (2) among other literary genres. There was academic and critical bias in "anthologies and literary histories, college texts and curricula, literary magazines, scholarly journals and critical histories" (2) against American drama, which was almost "written out of the American literary canon" because of the "culturally dominant puritan distaste for and suspicion of the theater" (3), while successful drama performances all over the country highlighted many unseen facets of identity presented through a "complicated genre that was and is socially created, distributed, experienced, and shared in a multiplicity of ways" (8). Introspection into identity profiles at thresholds is best at home within such a genre at periphery. Moreover, dramatic texts have an increased potential for interaction of identities given that dramas are written primarily to be performed; these performances are adapted 'responses' to the dramaturgy contextualized within specific circumstances. In the contemporary realm of ongoing contested, negotiated, recontextualized, and rewritten literary histories, American drama and theater have, as Thomas S. Hischak so aptly pointed out, become "as diverse and unmanageable as the country itself" (462) and demand equal attention with other cultural artifacts.

Due to its uncontested popularity, the dramatic genre remained on the main cultural road but at the edge of literary studies particularly and of American studies in general. In 2004, in the second edition of *Modern American Drama*, Bigsby remarked that American drama, irrespective of its acclaimed authors on the domestic and global stages, was enjoying a "casual disregard" (1) and was still treated with a condescending attitude on the part of the critical establishment. Bigsby's observation repeated his 1978 criticism on the marginal position of the American dramatic genre, when in a response to Walter Meserve's derogatory claims about the status of American drama, he pointed out that American dramas are as essential cultural paradigms as other literary or cultural manifestations. Dramas, unlike other literary genres, he wrote, functions as a present-time instrument measuring crucial and sometimes invisible changes in a given society and culture because the play is most sensitive to cultural and aesthetic shifts ("Drama as Cultural Sign" 331).

The theatrical metaphor is a useful tool for the interpretation of significant acts of culture. This rhetorical device became the basic concept used in the description of developmental phases of American studies: Gene Wise's "paradigm dramas" created the basic configuration of the cultural and institutional history of the field. The inherent quality of the dramatic metaphor suggests that there is a "dynamic image of ideas" (169) endowed with "trans-actional quality" which works to ensure a "continual dialogue" (169) in the field of American studies perceived as a extensive metaphorical 'stage' for various more or less dramatic encounters. This dialogue ensures the viability of the field, positing the dramatic paradigm at the heart of the discipline.

Drama is an exceptional space when it comes to what Mary Dudziak and Leti Volpp call "hydraulic relations" (598) in the crafting of identities. America, as Bigsby puts it, "immigrant country that it is," continues to be seen as a "contested space," in which identity is "constantly making and remaking itself" (*Modern American Drama* xi). In turn, American theater claims a part of this contested space and transfigures it from a border area into a dialogic contact zone of cultural mediation where issues of identity construction are revived, explored, publicly placed, and re-interpreted according to contemporary discursive and cultural practices. As Enikő Bollobás writes, after the Civil Rights Movements of the 1960s, American drama and histrionic arts took a radical turn: politics and identity coalesced in the theater of identity forming a cohesive tool for social change that had a cathartic effect which combined with a political mission has since served individuals and society alike (758).

In 2004, Shelley Fisher Fishkin evoked the arbitrariness of border spaces in her Presidential Address to the American studies Association entitled "Crossroads of Cultures: The Transnational Turn in American Studies." By starting her argument with Gloria Anzaldùa's ideas from *Borderlands/La Frontera*, Fishkin pointed out that the power of the borderland zone lies in its potential to transmute "the buzzing" of challenges into sites of "creative energy" (17). The problem of borders and borderlands has been a topic in permanent vogue not only in the frame of the American dramatic genre but also in the wider context of American studies. In the preface of the 2005 special issue of *American Quarterly* entitled *Legal Borderlands. Law and the Construction of American Borders*, Marita Sturken posed the "murky and complex" question involving "borders of and within identities" (v) in the context of an interdisciplinary approach to identity construction in contemporary America. The focus on marginal aspects of identity, alongside with other current methods of inquiry, diffuses previous constructions of American identities traditionally centered on mainstream heteronormativity that were, as Mary L. Dudziak and Leti Volpp wrote in the same *American Quarterly* issue, primarily "consolidated around the normal masculine through the casting out of perverse behavior" (600).

Albee's *The Goat or Who Is Sylvia?* and Vogel's *How I Learned to Drive* belong to this category of interrogating "perverse behavior" identities which, according to Fisher Fishkin, disrupt celebratory national narratives (19) or mainstream plots and add other possible ways of identity expression to the repertoire of culturally taboo subjects (for example, homosexuality and AIDS during the seventies and eighties).

In contemporary dramas, the strategy of reassessing identities necessarily opens up a space of real and symbolic transgression within what Dudziak and Volpp called the "internal American space" (595), a threshold of multiple accesses that made visible (or readable) within the synthetic monoculture of "normality," a topos that Akhil Gupta and James Fergusson named the "space[s] of ideological ambiguity" (qtd. in Dudziak and Volpp 596). As I wrote in "Borderlands: Postcolonial identities in American literature," these dramas, similar to other literary works, contain active, creative, contextual frames where identities not only "intersect, transfigure, and continually redefine each other" (41) but also, as Austin Sarat claimed, provide fertile terrains on which they are and can be "constructed, contested and made meaningful" (qtd. in Dudziak and Volpp 598).

Contemporary American drama inherited the practice of framing identities from a radical perspective. This revolutionary, pervasive concern with identity construction dates back to the 1960s, a decade of social and political imperatives which opened the way to many silenced voices, marginal discourses and invisible (or less visible) identities. During and after the 1960s a great number of literary texts by African Americans, women, gay and lesbian authors as well as literature by Native Americans, Latinos/Latinas, and Asian Americans appeared in a wide spectrum of publications. The Vietnam War also contributed to the enrichment of a body of texts pertaining to contemporary identity constructions in the United States written from a substantially different perspective from that of the mainstream community of canonized authors. The social and political changes of the sixties revealed in American dramas a close-to-genuine picture of identities, where "the freedom of becoming" was more powerful than what Bigsby called the "stasis of being" (*Modern American Drama* 267). Many post-sixties dramatic works in the United States depict starkly intimate and provocative themes—issues of sexuality, race and gender—all part of a genuine search for identity within a culture of raising voices.

Contemporary American dramas focus predominantly on the collapse of the nuclear family by exposing non-traditional family forms (Cristian 2006), as well as confused relationships between spouses and among family members; many plays offer close introspection into the taboo topics of pornography, prostitution, AIDS, homosexuality, sexual abuse, incest, and bestiality. This is what Bigsby calls the "theater of transformation" (2004b, 267), an exquisite form of theater in which identity is ensconced under the mask of 'normality' and stereotypes with the aim of showing how the pressure of tradition and social prejudice shapes individuals and the subsequent social performances of the subject. The plays of transformation depend on the very system they oppose; therefore they become essentially rebellious (268) and, as such, have a substantial potential for change.

The discussion of the chosen dramas has a double aim: to push forward a slice of the interpretive boundary of the dramatic genre into that of the larger discipline of American studies and to contribute to the body of textual challenge to mainstream critical stages of practice by providing another kind of interpretation to the current readings of America's unfolding identities. The thresholds of identity in *How I Learned to Drive* and *The Goat or Who Is Sylvia?* can be best surveyed through the figures of the protagonists. Vogel's main character is victimized by an incestuous desire and the play focuses on the behavioral uncertainties and on the sense of ambiguity resulting from an early sexual abuse that haunts the central character, whereas Albee's leading figure is involved in a love affair with an animal.

How I Learned to Drive charts a girl's journey through time that reflects the edges of her nascent identity and draws her profile through certain situations. The play delineates several delicate moments when the ambivalent feelings of the participating characters border on problematic behavioral patterns that result in an unmasked identity profile. Albee's play stretches the limits of human understanding and love both within and outside the framework of conventional marriage. Martin, the protagonist of *The Goat or Who Is Sylvia?*, tests the verges of acceptance in the domestic realm of his family and in the context of friendship. Both leading figures transgress the borders of expected social behavior. Their actions reflect displaced positions within family and society that ultimately lead to unfolding marginalized identities.

The intertextual inspiration for Paula Vogel's *How I Learned to Drive* was Vladimir Nabukov's *Lolita* (written in 1955 and unsuccessfully adapted by Edward Albee into dramatic form in 1981), David Mamet's *Oleanna* (1992) and the movie *To Kill a Mockingbird* (1962) directed by Robert Mulligan. As Bigsby claims, Vogel "touched the national nerve" (*Modern American Drama* 415) with her play in tackling the sensitive subject of abuse, incest, seduction and victimization. The choice of the topic places the author against the grain of so-called safe issues, fashionable at the end of the twentieth century America; with this drama she challenged, both existing "theatrical models and moral presumptions alike" (418). Lillian Hellman was the only significant representative of American women playwrights until the seventies; during the eighties and nineties the list expanded considerably, including Loraine Hansberry, Adrienne Kennedy, Ntozake Shange, Tina Howe, Marsha Norman, Suzan-Lori Parks, Wendy Wasserstein, Megan Terry, Maria Irene Fornes and many others. Paula Vogel currently joined the list and became one of the main literary spokesperson of women's identity crises in contemporary American drama.

Vogel's earlier plays, *Desdemona* (1979), *And Baby Makes Seven* (1984), *The Oldest Profession* (1988), *The Baltimore Waltz* (1992), *Hot 'N' Throbbing* (1993), and *The Mineola Twins* (1996) dealt with less traditional characters and unorthodox situations. Bigsby remarked that Vogel, while "aware of her own marginality, not least because she was not only a woman but an avowed lesbian" (*Modern American Drama* 411), was interested in works that provoked "negative empathy" (412). Accordingly, her first plays were either rejected by virtually all theaters they have been sent to, or had to wait years before they were finally produced.

The playwright, as Ann Pellegrini puts it, makes intimate connections with the "living edge of the past (another term for the 'psychic life')" in her dramas that hold "out the possibility of connecting otherwise, connecting with a difference" (474). Launched "in an indeterminate present" (482), *How I Learned to Drive* is constructed in cinematic flashbacks which gradually present, through the metaphor of driving lessons, the stages of sexual maturation and the progressive awakening of a young girl (nick)named Li'l Bit. She is the protagonist of the drama and also the narrating voice-over. Uncle Peck—named after Gregory Peck who played Atticus Finch in *To Kill a Mockingbird*—is the antagonist of the play and embodies a former war veteran, who is obsessed with his young relative, Li'l Bit, whom he teaches to drive in rural Maryland. He tries to keeps up the appearance of a happy marriage despite the fact that he is irresistibly drawn to the girl.

This disturbing dark comedy about hebephilia follows the route of Li'L Bit's puberty years and maps the points of her identity crisis revealed through several driving lessons. In an interview with Elizabeth Farnsworth on April 16th, 1998, Vogel commented about the stir the play had produced after its premiere at Off-Broadway's Vineyard Theater and emphasized that her drama was not only about the traumatic motifs of the Lolita syndrome. The playwright said that her text was about how the remembering and the voicing different moments of crisis can pave the way to solutions for traumas and stressed the importance of "healing, forgiving and moving on" (qtd. in Farnsworth 1998), all therapeutic strategies similar to the telling of women's oral histories.

The play's bittersweet tone and style as well as the open treatment of sexuality and the informal air of naivety recalling the innocent spirit of an Eden-like mythic space of encounter neighbors on the comic terrains of contemporary talk shows and television sit-coms. Nevertheless, this comic switch is deadly serious, as happens in most jokes. The naming of the characters in *How I Learned to Drive* is the first indication of the distress that lies at the bottom of the plot and the protagonist is the one that points out to its potential damage.

> LI'L BIT. In my family, folks tend to get nicknamed for their genita-
> lia. Uncle Peck for example. My mama's adage was "the titless won-
> der." [...] Even with my family background, I was sixteen or so be-
> fore I realized that pedophilia did not mean people who loved to bi-
> cycle. (12-13)

The adult Li'l Bit relocates the objects and the movements of her own car that connect her to the traumatic, past stories behind each item. The radio, the fuel tank, the tires, the doors, the key, the seatbelt, the dashboard, the side, and especially the rearview mirror, are all checkpoints, borders, milestones of her identity construction. She is able to build and rebuild her identity later only in relation to these objects. Li'l Bit's sexuality is symboli-cally located between gear shifts and speed limits; she extracts her behavior-al patterns from driving rules and makes up new signifying practices in a drama of her own, where Uncle Peck becomes a passive observer and, fi-nally, a victim of his own desires. The material inventory of the car is both a psychic projection and a landmark of Li'l Bit's development; she shapes her identity by remembering and reassessing these objects and the function they have. Among the most traumatic ones is the radio through which she evokes the music she used to hear while learning to drive.

> LI'L BIT. [...] The nearest sensation I feel—of flight in the body—I
> guess I feel when I'm driving. On a day like today. It's five A.M. The
> radio says it's going to be clear and crisp. I've got five hundred miles
> of highway ahead of me—and some back roads too. I filled the tank
> last night, and had the oil checked. Checked the tyres, too. You've
> got to treat her... with respect. First thing I do is: Check under the
> car. To see if any two year olds or household cats have crawled be-
> neath, and strategically placed their skulls behind my back tires. (*Li'l
> Bit crouches*). Nope. Then I get in the care. (*Li'l Bit does so*). I lock the
> doors. And turn the key. Then I adjust the most important control
> on the dashboard—the radio— [...] Ahh. (*Beat.*) I adjust my seat. Fas-
> ten my seatbelt. Then I check the right side mirror—check the left
> side. (*She does.*) (58-59)

Li'l Bit's story exhibits her delicate facets of identity: she appears both as a grown-up woman and a naïve "little" girl. As an adult person she is aware of the cause of her present identity problems and acknowledges herself as a woman in full control of not only the car she drives but also of her body and life. It takes a long time to understand and bridge past things. Li'l Bit is already 35-year-old when she starts recalling her first driving lessons which took place when she was ten. The protagonist-narrator remembers the se-ducer-victim set-up of her driving hours and by remembering it she acknowledge its traumatic content. "That day was the last day I lived in my body" (59), Li'l Bit says, emphasizing that afterwards she "retreated above the neck," and lived inside the "fire" in her head ever since (58). Since she has 'lost' the innocence of her body, the protagonist substitutes it with an external object, a car. The automobile she drives as an adult becomes the metaphor of her symbolically mutilated body that cannot 'live' below the neck. Similar to the role of a character in a drama, this unnamed car model represents not only the carcass of her past but also the instrument of her future liberation. At the end of the drama what Li'l Bit sees in the rearview mirror is not the lingering history of guilty distress that haunts her into continuously looking back but an objective past she recovered and used to gain freedom. By talking about her escapades involving Uncle Peck there is also an additional release of tension: the glimpse back becomes a memory of learning rather than a traumatic episode. Through it Li'l Bit learns how to relate her body to the pleasures of driving rather than to any previous sexual harassment. The trauma is finally expelled and she reaches the safe boundaries of her new identity: the new woman now knows how to protect herself by fastening the seat belt and adjusting not only her driver's seat but also her entire self into a position that shifts from that of the learner to that of the power holder.

Vogel, as Bigsby remarks, is keen to remind her audience of the "arbitrariness of the lines drawn by society," because "[W]hat is legitimate at eighteen is statutory rape at the age of seventeen" (*Contemporary American Playwrights* 322). The issue of the boundaries and lines is clearly (im)posed by the child Li'l Bit in *How I Learned to Drive*. Once she tells Uncle Peck: "[…] You've got to let me—draw the line. And once it's drawn, you mustn't cross it" (47). Nevertheless, he disregards any prohibitions and enters the girl's personal and intimate space, transgressing the voiced but invisible lines of restrictions despite Li'l Bit warning. She is not passive and realizes the dangers of crossing symbolic borders when she tells Uncle Peck that "You have—you have gone way over the line" (54). This "way over the line" will lead her into building new frames of identity later.

Li'l Bit's personality undergoes several changes as she grows from the stage of innocence symbolized by the learner status during the driving lessons to adulthood. The demarcation lines between the stages of this symbolic development are like gear changes showing the stages of the protagonist's development at the threshold of childhood and maturity, at the rough edges of questions and answers. Gradually she goes from first to second gear, then to the reverse gear and neutral gear until she reaches full maturity, represented in the play by the grown-up woman's use of automatic gear.

Vogel's surrealist approach in *How I Learned to Drive* maps the crucial points of the development of Li'l Bit identity. She is entangled in the web of an incestuous relationship, which harmful as it is, secures her a safe passage. In this double-edged situation the main character finds a unique voice and builds an identity out of taboos and silenced topics. As Pellegrini writes, she cannot and is not even willing to escape her memories and her past that is her burden and her gift (482). Jill Dolan remarked that this drama, which is cast in a "rather sadly nostalgic, presentational yet nuanced style" is at the same time "moving and liberating" (498) for Li'l Bit, who arrives finally in charge of her own car, her own body on an open road of possibilities.

Vogel makes not only her protagonist but also the audience subject to what Bigsby saw as a "constant reassessment of their attitude towards the characters" and by doing so the playwright disturbs "earlier assumptions and make[s] the observer aware of his or her shifting moral perspective" (*Modern American Drama* 417). With this drama, the author performs a morally challenging journey; she explores and integrates lives that are "tangential to the thrust of her society" (329) and exposes problematic edges of identity by making visible the volatile nature of compulsory lines drawn by the society and the unforeseen effects these metaphorical frontiers might involve.

In *The Goat or Who is Sylvia? (Notes Toward a Definition of Tragedy)* the spotlight is on "affective 'primordial' and familial bonds" (Somerville 660) that radically change the lives of the characters. The play—recalling Aristotle's *Poetics*, Friedrich Nietzsche's *The Birth of Tragedy* and Shakespeare's *The Two Gentlemen of Verona*—divided critics and reviewers alike because it focused on a bizarre question about the nature of love. Love is hidden behind the mask of identity search, which gradually develops around the tropes of a dysfunctional family, gender issues and bestiality.

The subject of *The Goat or Who is Sylvia?* is, according to Ellen J. Gainor (who quotes the playwright), "about the few remaining taboos" (204) in our society and was written, as Charles McNulty has aptly pointed out, to "test the tolerance of the audience" (2002). For doing so, Gainor concluded, Albee "calculatedly used bestiality as an aberration to make homosexuality appear normal by comparison" (200). As Albee pointed out in a collection of occasional pieces entitled *Stretching My Mind*, bestiality is indeed "discussed during the play (as is flower arranging) but is a generative matter rather than the 'subject'" which is rather the issue of love and loss along with "the limits of our tolerance and who, indeed, we are" (262). Albee initially wanted to write a drama about the AIDS epidemic combined with a case of suicide but this plot did not make it to the page or to the stage; instead, he created *The Goat or Who Is Sylvia?*, which reflected the playwright's initial thoughts on

> the limits of our tolerance of the behavior of others than ourselves, especially when such behavior ran counter to what we believed to be acceptable social and moral boundaries, and our willingness to imagine ourselves behaving in such an unacceptable fashion—in other words our refusal to imagine ourselves subject to circumstances outside our own comfort zones. (*Stretching My Mind* 259)

The critics' response to this thespian endeavor was controversial. While Elysa Gardner denounced the play as "nauseating" (qtd. in Gainor 203), Clive Barnes saw it as "one of the wittiest and funniest plays Albee has ever written" (qtd. in Gainor 204). These divisive critical assessments reflected "discomfort," "hostility" and showed little tolerance on the part of viewers and readers. This critical attitude also demonstrated the fact that the play-wright, as Gainor insisted, had "created a dramatic world whose actions and concerns could be neither avoided nor dismissed" (204). According to Enikő Bollobás, Albee's dramas deal directly with delicate issues involving marginal identities, where the dramatic conflicts are centered mostly around the parent-child relationships that portray sharp and, in many cases, eccentric antagonisms at work within and outside the domestic realm (753).

In *The Goat or Who is Sylvia?* the plotline shifts from the structural frames of the traditional family and human liaisons to the world of fauna and to bestial relations. This unusual dramatic setting conceals a special conflict that tests the general boundary of love and the limits of human relationships involving family and friendship. The plot is about the love story of Martin, the protagonist, and a real goat named Sylvia. Such a lurid configuration of characters had not existed previously in animal stories from Albee's earlier dramas. For example, in *The Zoo Story* (1959) the aggressive love-hate relationship between Jerry and the landlady's unfriendly black dog was not as much about poisoning the animal as a game centered on the issue of miscommunication between participants in order to achieve appropriate communication; *A Delicate Balance* (1966) tackled, among other issues, animal euthanasia within the realm of changed affection and in the satire-fantasy *Seascape* (1975), the human-sized lizard-therianthropes Leslie and Sarah, were subjects of almost supernatural transgression as they practiced shapeshifting.

Unlike these animal allegories, *The Goat or Who Is Sylvia?* depicts categories of dominant culture and forces readers—in a way akin to Vogel's play—to rethink these norms in a dramatic context in which it is extremely difficult to make, as Gainor writes, "clear-cut distinctions among the manifold, polymorphously perverse expressions of sexual desire" (213). In addition, as Steven Bottoms writes, in this story of marital infidelity, homosexuality and bestiality that Albee destabilizes not only the epistemology but also "the very ontology of the stage world we are watching (where *are* we; what world *is* this?)" (14). *The Goat or Who Is Sylvia?* unveils an unusual liaison within which boundaries have been pushed far enough. Accordingly, Gainor suggests this drama be interpreted as an extensive work of social criticism stretching from the classical era through the modernist theater tradition to that of the contemporary problem plays (211-212).

The plot of Albee's problem play is simple: Martin and Stevie, a couple of 'tragic' characters are seemingly happy with their successful lives and mundane habits of upper class Americans. They have been together for twenty-two years and have a seventeen-year-old "funny son" (*The Goat, or Who Is Sylvia?* 77) son, Billy, who is gay "as the nineties" (21). Homosexuality is neither a taboo in this play nor the source of any domestic conflict. Epitomes of a liberal society, Stevie and Martin accept their son as he is; Martin even declares his parental approval when he laconically says to Billy that "[Y]ou're gay, and that's fine" (48).

Similar to Albee's other married characters such as Mummy and Daddy in *The American Dream* (1961), Martha and George in *Who's Afraid of Virginia Woolf?* (1962), Agnes and Tobias in *A Delicate Balance* (1966), She and He in *Counting the Ways* (1976), Gillian and Jack in *Marriage Play* (1987), or Girl and Boy in *The Play About the Baby* (1998), only to mention a few examples, the marriage of Stevie and Martin is at a crucial point, in serious crisis. Martin, the fifty-year-old award-winning architect in *The Goat, or Who Is Sylvia?*, feels a "misfit" (75) and is deeply alienated from the urban artificialities, and the superficial and hypocritical world of twentieth-century corporate capitalism with intense consumerism that surrounds him. He perceives himself as devoid of any vital substance and tries to find refuge in looking for another house outside the city, as if a switch of home could help him restart his life. As he walks in the countryside in search of a weekend farmhouse, Martin unexpectedly comes across a she-goat with whom he falls instantly in love. He anthropomorphizes the goat by naming her Sylvia after the Roman goddess of the forest and moon, transforming her into his pastoral ideal. Their short but intensive intimacy makes Martin reevaluate his former, misrepresented identity that almost vanished while unconditionally living by the values and rules of the urban, post-industrial society. Martin describes his detour from the grey, mundane days as a journey into an Arcadian realm, an exotic territory, a terrain with no boundaries and limitations, where he can submerge into the unfamiliar, into something that cannot be related to anything known to him before. In a tensed dialogue he has with Stevie, Martin confesses the circumstances and the ecstatic frenzy of his sexual encounter with Sylvia, the goat:

> MARTIN. And I was driving out of the town, back to the highway, and I stopped at the top of a hill [...] And I stopped, and the view was... wonderful. Not spectacular, but wonderful—fall, the leaves turning [...] I stopped and got us things—vegetables and things. [...] And it was then that I saw her. [...] And I closed the trunk of the car, with all that I'd gotten—*(pause)*... it was then that I saw her. And she was looking at me... with those eyes. [...] And what I felt was... it was unlike anything I'd ever felt before. It was so... amazing. There she was. [...] She was looking at me with those eyes of hers

and… I melted, I think. I think that's what I did: I melted. […] I'd never seen such an expression. It was pure… and trusting and… and innocent; so… so guileless. […] I… I went to where she was—to the fence where she was, and I knelt there, eye level…
STEVIE. (*Quiet loathing*) Goat level.
MARTIN. […] It was as if an alien came out for whatever it was, and it … took me with it, and it was… and ecstasy and a purity, and a… love of a… (*dogmatic*) un-i-mag-in-able kind, and it relates to nothing *whatever*, to nothing that can be *related* to! Don't you see? Don't you see the… don't you see the "thing" that happened to me? What nobody understands? Why I can't feel what I'm supposed to!? Because it relates to nothing? It can't have happened! It did, but it can't have! (*Stevie shakes her head*) […] (79-81)

Martin's friend, Ross, disgusted, unmasks this idyllic love and questions the limits of his friendship with Martin by writing the truth to Stevie. Ross, as Gainor explains, wants to save Martin's public self by rescuing his private life (211). Nevertheless, Martin challenges other boundaries, too: he puts to test the father-son relationship and pushes it to the edges of a pseudo-Oedipal crisis bordering on incest.

Outraged by the object of her husband's love and exasperated by the prospects the liaison with Sylvia can bring, Stevie puts an end to her husband's passionate affair in an act where, in Gainor's vision, Eros and Thanatos collide (213): as a raving maenad, she kills Sylvia in an almost mystic act of ritual murder. Sylvia-the-goat thus becomes the *tragos*, the scapegoat who has been sacrificed for past sins and as a lesson for future. With her deed, Stevie forces the alienated Martin back where she thinks he belongs: to the traditional cosmic order symbolized, as Gainor pointed out, by the Great Chain of Being (214) and to the conventional social and domestic domain.

It seems that established regulations do not and will not apply to this dysfunctional family. In this play, Martin remains uncertain of his newly imposed limits when he claims: "I don't know that there are any rules for where we are" (97). Billy arrives to a similar, "emotionally devastating conclusion" (Albee qtd. in Gainor 204) when he realizes that his family is "beyond all the rules" (98). His final questions, "Dad? Mom?" (110)—the last line of the drama—suggest an imperative need for what Gainor calls the renegotiation of roles (214) leading to new definitions of identity.

Martin reassembles himself in a moment of crisis: from a prominent architect and a model husband, he becomes an infamous family man who has known the calling of the wild. He knows that his identity quest requires sacrifice; therefore he succumbs to the tragic situation hoping that his deed, ultimately, will find understanding. In this context, Sylvia becomes a true scapegoat that can 'save' Martin, who will begin to know once more his limitations and questions identity not where it stops being visible but where identity starts acting itself out.

In *The Goat or Who Is Sylvia?* the protagonist's identity is constructed as emerging from the nuclear family model, which is destroyed by the protagonist's inability to cope with the rigid paradigms of increasingly stressful factors generated by an urban, metropolitan culture in tandem with social expectations. Martin is similar to the character of Yank in Eugene O'Neil's *The Hairy Ape* (1922). Yank is compared to a hairy ape, goes to a zoo to see a gorilla, and enters the cage to embrace the animal. He finally understands his outcast place in the society only in the fatal embrace of the beast. Martin, Albee's alienated protagonist, finds a kindred being with whom he finally builds his identity. Nevertheless, Martin is doomed to live in the permanent embrace of the consequences of his love affair with Sylvia, the goat. Unlike O'Neill, whose character is punished for his transgressive act, Albee confronts the dominant culture with its own designation of alternative love and challenges this very culture to rethink, as Gainor pointed out, its "clear-cut distinctions among the manifold, polymorphously perverse expressions of sexual desire" (213).

The American theater has undergone significant changes in the presentation and discussion of dynamic identity constructions in comparison with the emerging theaters of identity in the 1960s and 1970s. As Harris Smith has shown, American drama (and theater) has "mirrored peculiarly American social, political, and historical issues in traditional as well as challenging forms and experimental styles" reflecting a "forum for a plurality of voices" (9). This genre has been a "reflexive cultural barometer" that has responded to "national and regional problems, either in reifying prevailing sentiments or by challenging dominant ideologies" (9). In the past few decades, an increasing number of playwrights from America's political, racial and gender margins are more open and daring with the most radical subjects. Bigsby remarked that the dilemma and the strength of the American theater lies in these very peculiar cultural acts presenting multiple identities at play in a plural country that is subject to a continuous process of transformation:

> The blandness, the anonymity, the conformity which was America's gift as well as its burden was now to be met with a determination to reach back beyond homogenizing myths to a self and a group identity which had their origins in other times and other places. The result was a transformed society [...] The making of America has never ended. That is its dilemma and its strength [...] The theatre, likewise, is never complete. It, too, requires the collaborative efforts of those who bring to the same stage experiences which differ radically. (*Modern American Drama* 361)

According to Howard Sherman, Vogel does not write, nor intends to create thesis plays; for her, theater is a place of public discourse, a threshold ground where maverick voices must be made heard (2004). Theater, Sherman continues, is in Vogel's opinion about confronting serious issues, especially if those go astray from the main borders of social discourses and that is why she prefers writing plays that are upsetting and disturbing (2004). Albee also has shaped, and still does, a theater that goes further beyond, ultimately, the daring enterprise of Vogel. Albee said that he is interested in writing works that "shake[s] people up, and make them change in some way" (qtd. in Bottoms 249). He laconically calls this militant call to transformation, "playwriting" (249).

Vogel's and Albee's works exhibit radical experiences and portray unusual character profiles through a mode of transgressive writing generating a threshold territory of creative energies, a no man's land of unusual identity constructions where figural or real borders are arbitrary ongoing modifications. Both Vogel and Albee interrogate facets of complex and sometimes extremely difficult questions concerning identities and identity crises in contemporary American culture and society but without imposing any value judgments or creating moralizing conclusions. Their plays are probably the best to expose those special cultural signs that echo the arbitrariness of certain limitations by depicting problematic identity positions at the thresholds. If seen in a larger frame, these plays are, as many other important episodes in the development of a culture, representative acts dramatizing inherent possibilities in a given cultural situation, acts which spotlight what Wise saw in his influential "Paradigm Dramas in American Studies" as "changing boundaries of what is possible for a person or a group at a particular time and in a particular place and in a particular milieu" (169). They can thus be considered sample "paradigm dramas" of cultural experience that accurately exhibit the current aims and critical imperatives of New American studies.

Works Cited

Albee, Edward. (1965). "The Zoo Story." *Absurd Drama*, Introduction by Martin Esslin. Harmondsworth: Penguin, 157-185. Print.

---. (1969). *A Delicate Balance*. Harmondsworth: Penguin. Print.

---. (1975). *Seascape: A Play*. New York: Atheneum. Print.

---. (2003). *The Goat, or Who Is Sylvia? (Notes Toward a Definition of Tragedy)*. Woodstock & New York: Overlook. Print.

---. (2005). "About this Goat." *Stretching My Mind*. New York: Carroll and Graf Publishers. Print.

Bigsby, C.W.E. (1978). "Drama as Cultural Sign: American Dramatic Criticism, 1945-1978." *American Quarterly* 30. 3 (September): 331-57. Print.

---. (2004 a). *Contemporary American Playwrights*. Cambridge: Cambridge University Press. Print.

---. (2004 b). *Modern American Drama: 1945-2000*. Cambridge: Cambridge University Press. Print.

Bollobás, Enikő. (2005). *Az amerikai irodalom története*. Budapest: Osiris. Print.

Bottoms, Stephen. (2005). "Borrowed Time: An Interview with Edward Albee." *The Cambridge Companion to Edward Albee*. Ed. Steven Bottoms. Cambridge: Cambridge University Press, 231-52. Print.

Cristian, Réka M. (2005). "Borderlands: Postcolonial Identities in Contemporary American Literature." *Theory and Practice 4: Proceedings from the Eighth Conference of English, American and Canadian Studies (Literature and Cultural Studies)*. Ed. Jan Chovanec. Brno: Masaryk University, 35-42. Print.

---. (2006). "From Delicate Absence to Presence: The Child in Edward Albee's Alternating Families." *AMERICANA E-Journal of American Studies in Hungary*, Vol. II. Nr. 2. Fall. Web. Retrieved from http://americanaejournal.hu/vol2no2/cristian-essay. Access: January 7, 2007.

Dudziak, Mary L., and Leti Volpp. (2005). "Introduction. Legal Borders: Law and the Construction of American Borders." *American Quarterly* 57. 3 (September): 593-610. Print.

Dolan, Jill. (2005). "Lesbian and Gay Drama." *Twentieth-Century American Drama*. Ed. David Krassner. Malden, MA: Blackwell, 486-503. Print.

Farnsworth, Elizabeth. (1998). "PBS interview with Paula Vogel, April 16, 1998." Web. Retrieved from: http://www.pbs.org/newshour/bb/entertainment/jan-june98/play_4-16.html. Access: September 22, 2006.

Fishkin, Shelley Fisher. (2005). "Crossroads of Cultures: The Transnational Turn in American Studies—Presidential Address to the American Studies Association November 12, 2004." *American Quarterly* 57. 1 (March): 17-57. Print.

Gainor, Ellen J. (2005). "Albee's *The Goat*: Rethinking Tragedy for the 21st Century." *The Cambridge Companion to Edward Albee*. Ed. Stephen Bottoms. Cambridge: Cambridge University Press, 199-216. Print.

Hischak, Thomas S. (2001). *American Theatre: A Chronicle of Comedy and Drama*. Oxford: Oxford University Press. Print.

McNulty, Charles. (2002). "Edward Albee's Domestic Animals. After a Flurry of Productions, a Critical Look at an American Master." *The Village Voice*. May 21. Web. Retrieved from www.villagevoice.com/issues/0221/mcnulty.php. Access: May 28, 2002.

O'Neill, Eugene. (1994). "The Hairy Ape." *The Heath Anthology of American Literature*, (Second Edition), Vol. 2, Gen. ed. Paul Lauter. Lexington, Mass.: D.C. Heath and Company, 1332-1363. Print.

Pellegrini, Ann. (2005). "Repercussions and Remainders in the Plays of Paula Vogel: An Essay in Five Moments." *Twentieth-Century American Drama*. Ed. David Krassner. Malden, MA: Blackwell, 473-485. Print.

Sherman, Howard. (2004). "Signature Theatre Company, Playwrights in Residence: Interview with Paula Vogel on November 26, 2004." Web. Retrieved from: http://www.americantheatrewing.org/downstagecenter/detail/paula_vogel. Access: October 1, 2006.

Somerville, Siobhan B. (2005). "Notes Toward a Queer History of Naturalization." *American Quarterly* 57. 3 (September): 659-75. Print.

Smith, Susan Harris. (2006). *American Drama. The Bastard Art.* Cambridge: Cambridge Univeresity Press. Print.

Sturken, Marita. (2005). "Preface." *American Quarterly* 57. 3 (September): v-vi. Print.

Vogel, Paula. (1998). *How I Learned to Drive.* New York: Dramatists Play Service. Print.

Wise, Gene. (1999). "Paradigm Dramas in American Studies: A Cultural and Institutional History of the Movement." *Locating American Studies. The Evolution of a Discipline.* Ed. Lucy Maddox. Baltimore: The Johns Hopkins University Press, 166-210. Print.

3. Sites of Identity Through Cinematic Vistas

3.1. Adaptation, Auteurship, and Identity

The second part of this e-book discusses identity constructions through cinematic vistas. This part is subdivided into two sections: "Adaptation, Auteurship, and Identity," which centers on extradiegetic identity issues pertaining to filmic authorship; the "Negotiation, Characters, and Identity" part shows samples of intradiegetic identities caught in cross-cultural negotiations.

The first section, "Adaptation, Auteurship, and Identity," contains two essays, which deal with the construction of author/auteur identities through the intricate processes of film adaptation. The first text, *"The Roman Springs of Mrs. Stone.* Auteurship in José Quintero's and Robert Allan Ackerman's Adaptations of Tennessee Williams's Novel" is an incursion into how Tennessee Williams connects the world of literature with that of the film by managing to make his own name on the Broadway as playwright and later in Hollywood, where he exerted a major influence on the forms and history of American commercial filmmaking. The analysis of the auteurial function in the two film versions of his novel, *The Roman Spring of Mrs. Stone,* directed first by José Quintero and then by Robert Alland Ackerman, show how the name of the novel's author pervades both filmic discourses and generates, though gender shifts and variable character correlations, an ideological continuity and a identity that materializes in the complex forms of the implied auteur and auteur.

The second essay of the "Adaptation, Auteurship, and Identity" section, "Who's Afraid of Adapting Albee? Synergic Auteurship in *Who's Afraid of Virginia Woolf?"* focuses on the identity of the filmic auteur(s) of in Mike Nichols's film adaptation of Edward Albee's *Who's Afraid of Virginia Woolf?*

showing that here the identity of the auteur shifts from the rigid notion of the director as enounced by the Americanization of the auteur theory towards a synergic auteur function involving multiple auteurs, including the playwright himself.

3.1.1. The Roman Springs of Mrs. Stone.
Auteurship in José Quintero's and Robert Allan Ackerman's
Adaptations of Tennessee Williams's Novel

> The sign of a clever auteur is to achieve the illusion that there is a sole
> individual responsible for magnificent creations that require thousands of
> people to accomplish.
> *Louis Mayer*

Tennessee Williams's work pivoted around the implicit figure of the author especially through his dramatic poet characters—Tom Wingfield in *The Glass Menagerie* (1944), Allan Grey in *A Streetcar Named Desire* (1947), Sebastian Venable in *Suddenly Last Summer* (1958), and Jonathan Coffin in *The Night of the Iguana* (1962). Nevertheless, as R. Barton Palmer and William R. Bray claim, he managed to make his own name on the Broadway as playwright and later in Hollywood, where he exerted a major influence on the forms and history of American commercial filmmaking (viii), becoming today a household name in American culture. By centering on and deconstructing postwar issues of gender and sexuality, Williams's dramas, according to Matthew C. Roudané, "reinvented the American stage" (2) on the Broadway stages and provided American filmmaking with works that were sources for a new kind of "adult, naughty" (8) movies that became the classic Williams films famous for outwitting the practice of film censorship.

After the success of his dramas on Broadway, Tennessee Williams became one of the most frequently adapted playwrights in Hollywood, and, as Palmer and Bray write, a "movie-made playwright" (15) credited in many cases as the screenplay writer and co-screenwriter of his drama adaptations to film. Alongside dramatic works, Williams's poems, short stories and his one novel, *The Roman Spring of Mrs. Stone* (1950), also contributed to the creation of a specific cultural discourse of alterity on the page, on the stage and on screen, a Williamesque world that has since become an organic part of the American collective cultural vocabulary (7). This world is marked by what Jurij Tinyanov calls "idiosyncratic" style (5-25) that discloses those specific markers Michel Foucault named "shifters" (205) that are emblematic of Tennessee Williams's oeuvre thus marking the trade name of the author.

According to Foucault, the author's name marks the general frames of a person's texts by revealing a unique, personalized "mode of being" (202). The name of the author as cohesive device is one of the most relevant tools for mapping trademark patterns in a pool of various texts. The name indicates both the status of the writer and the person's textual discourse within a given society and culture (202). Most literary texts are endowed with an author-function that assists their understanding and contextualization: for example, contemporary theories of gender and postcolonialism tend to revive, as Bence Nánay has shown, the figure producing the work of art (15) by focusing on descriptive cultural constructions of authorial attributes.

In film theory, the notion of the author correlates with the filmic author or auteur. According to Susan Hayward, the auteur—as in Foucault's definition—is an ideological figure who emerges from the construction of his or her own films (26). The analogy between the literary author and the filmic auteur began to be acknowledged during the first and second decades of the twentieth century and was a key feature of the German *Autorenfilm* [author film] that conferred upon the writer of the movie script the authority over the entire film. Later, the concept of the movie authorship was restricted to the name of the filmmaker. In *Le Cinéma et les letters modernes*, Jean Epstein compared the cinematic techniques of filmmakers D.W. Griffith and Sergei Eisenstein to the literary tropes of Gustave Flaubert and Charles Dickens by describing, as I wrote in *Enounters of the Filmic Kind*, salient correspondences between the literary and filmic narratives (64). Later, Alexandre Astruc emphasized the analogy between authorship in literature and authorship in film by considering filmmakers as visual artists metaphorically 'writing' with light. For Astruc, the writer's pen (*stylo*) in the case of filmmaking became the camera-pen (*camera stylo*) of the director as individual artist (64).

As Pam Cook writes, the Americanization of the auteur theory adapted and expanded the idea of Alexandre Astruc's *camera stylo* fused with that of the *politiques des auteurs* as elaborated in the French *Cahiers du Cinema* (119) during the 1950s and claimed (Hollywood) film directors to be *par excellence* auteurs. This theory was challenged not only by Pauline Kael's harsh criticism but also by post-structuralist theories that questioned the subject(s) producing the meaning(s) of the filmic text. As a result, the director as the main source of auteurship lost its quasi-totalitarian position and the concept of the auteur has become subject to a plurality of approaches.

Today the auteur function presents itself in a similar manner to what Andrew Sarris described as a "pattern in constant flux" (517) but not in the rigid sense Sarris considered. The flux is not about the rise and fall of names and directors or a canonization process: the auteur theory has simply shifted from the single auteur concept toward a more inclusive and less rigid paradigm. Contemporary theories of filmic auteurship de-center the director of a movie as a single creative entity in filmmaking to allow for a more practical concept of the auteur-function, which, as Hayward (26-27) and Nánay (18-19) claim, enables a more authentic approach to film authorship. This concept of the author-function in literature is a complex notion shedding light on various modes of authorship. Among these, as described by Wayne C. Booth in *The Rhetoric of Fiction*, is the "author contained;" it appears as a special category of authorial function and denotes an abstract subject displaying the "intricate relationship of the so-called real author with his various official versions of himself" (71), pointing to the concept of the implied author. In some cases, the implied author embodies the real author but the term can also refer to a virtual person who sometimes is a fictional narrator or a character representing a peculiar point of view, ideology or world-view. Most often, the implied author denotes an intermediary position based on the theoretical compromise established between the figure of the real author as envisaged in traditional biography criticism and the actual narrative voice of the literary text similar to a film star's "persona" which consists of what Christine Gledhill coined as the "real" person or off-screen individual and the "reel" figure or the character on the screen (qtd. in Hayward 352). In "Is There an 'Implied' Author in Every Film?," Booth revisited the issue of the implied author in an essay about the *American Beauty* (1999, dir. Sam Mendes) where he stated that every good film needs to have an implied author, an implied center, a true voice among the conglomerate of voices present in the making of a movie. If a literary text can have an implied author besides the author, then, by analogy, a film can also have an implied auteur as an implied center besides the auteur. The function of the implied auteur is equivalent to that of the author contained in the works of fiction and represents an authorial function positioned between the ideological figure of the auteur and the actual voice of the filmic narrative.

But what happens with the literary author-functions in film adaptations? Do shifters change with the transition from the literary work to film? What about the change of shifters from one movie to the other? What is behind the difference between the two adaptations of the same literary work? In this chapter I will examine the interplay between the literary author-function with the subsequent auteur-functions in two film adaptations based on Tennessee Williams's only novel, *The Roman Spring of Mrs. Stone*. The first adaptation of this fiction to the big screen was directed by José

Quintero in 1961 (with the alternative title *The Widow and the Gigolo*); the second one, directed by Robert Allan Ackerman in 2003, was produced for television.

José Quintero and Robert Allan Ackerman are not considered auteurs in the classical sense of the term; both of them are primarily theatre directors directing motion pictures made for television. Quintero's most important adaptations include *Windows* (1955 TV), *Medea* (1959 TV), *Our Town* (1959 TV), *The Roman Spring of Mrs. Stone* (1961), and *A Moon for the Misbegotten* (1975 TV), while Ackerman's filmography consists of *Mrs. Cage* (1992 TV), *David's Mother* (1994 TV), *Safe Passage* (1994 TV), *Suddenly* (1996 TV), *Passion's Way* (1997 TV), *Outrage* (1998 TV), *Forget Me Never* (1999 TV), *Double Platinum* (1999 TV), *Baby* (2000 TV), *Life with Judy Garland: Me and My Shadows* (2001 TV), *The Reagans* (2003 TV), *The Roman Spring of Mrs. Stone* (2003 TV) and *The Ramen Girl* (2008), among many others. In terms of the auteur question, both adaptations of *The Roman Spring of Mrs. Stone* remain subject to further investigation.

In terms of adaptation, the most important antecedent of *The Roman Spring of Mrs. Stone* was *A Streetcar Named Desire* (1947) directed by Elia Kazan in 1951. Tennessee Williams, the author of the drama, was also the co-screenwriter (with Oscar Saul) of this movie that changed the rules of censorship represented by the Production Code Administration (PCA). The result was a new type of Hollywood film: *A Streetcar Named Desire* became the first adult art movie in America, signaling the beginning of the commercial American art cinema that presented, as Palmer writes, "startling differences from the standard Hollywood movie in the representation of sexual themes" (216). Unlike other famous playwrights, Tennessee Williams became "central to the history of the American commercial theatre" and played "a significant role in the development of the postwar American cinema" (205) because his literary work was the key source "in the development of an 'adult' form of cinematic entertainment, one radically different from the standard studio fare of the Hollywood boom" (210). Similar to the Kazan's version of Williams's drama, the 1961 big screen adaptation of the *The Roman Spring of Mrs. Stone* employed analogous adult components concerning sexuality and gender issues. Forty-two years later, the Ackerman version was also subject to strict rating procedures by the Motion Picture Association of America (MPAA) and was rated "R" (containing some adult material) for sexuality and nudity by the film rating system.

By the time the first film version of *The Roman Spring of Mrs. Stone* was made, the movie industry was moving beyond the sensational type of eroticism displayed by the first American adult film studios which tended to favor "more graphic presentations of the human body and of sexual connection" in comparison with which Williams's cinematic world appeared, in Palmer's and Bray's formulation as old-fashioned failing to "connect with audiences" (xii). According to Brenda Murphy, the 1961 version produced by A. A. Productions and Seven Arts-Warner Bros. was a "major flop" (200), but Williams, who was never satisfied with the adaptation of his works, defended Quintero's version and emphasized that *The Roman Spring of Mrs. Stone*, "the last important work of both Miss Leigh and of the director José Quintero," was "a poem" (qtd. in Murphy 200). With this metaphor, which alludes to an accomplished fidelity to the original work, the playwright also emphasized the movie's art qualities crediting auteurship to both the star and the director of the film. Furthermore, as Laura Fries shows, in the 2003 Showtime Networks adaptation, Ackerman and screenplay writer Martin Sherman became "worthy caretakers" of Williams's novel because they produced a film that "rang truer" to the Williams text than the previous version which reflected a fidelity to the letter rather than to the spirit of the novel. Although this adaptation was nominated for two Golden Globes and five Emmy Awards, it had partial success winning only one Golden Globe Award for the best performance (Helen Mirren) in motion pictures made for television.

The raw material for these film adaptations is a short novel about a middle-aged famous actress, Karen Stone, whose wealthy husband dies on their way to Italy. After the death of her husband, Karen decides to stay in Rome, where she falls prey to carnal desire. She "drifts" into a relationship with a young handsome Italian *marchetta*, Paolo di Leo, her paid male companion. Williams portrays Karen in a manner recalling Somerset Maugham's actress Julia Lambert in *The Theatre* (1934) where Julia fights time, loves and lovers. *The Roman Spring of Mrs. Stone* also recalls the misty temptations of Henry James's *Daisy Miller* (1878) and the erotic impulses of Thomas Mann's *Death in Venice* (1912), the dangerous affairs of Anthony Burns in Tennessee Williams's short story *Desire and the Black Masseur* (1948) and the mysterious circumstances of Sebastian Venable's violent death in *Suddenly Last Summer* (1958). The trope of the senescent actress in search of love is perennial in Williams's dramatic oeuvre. Karen Stone's is a prototype for Williams's the pantheon of aging stars and prima donnas embodied by the character of Alexandra del Lago Princess Kosmonopolis in *Sweet Bird of Youth* (1961), who falls in love with the young opportunist Chance Wayne, and Sissy Flora Goforth in *The Milktrain Doesn't Stop Here Anymore* (1964), who dies with the help of handsome Chris Flanders nicknamed the Angel of Death.

Williams's novel is divided into three parts: "A Cold Sun," "Island, Island!" and "The Drift." The first part introduces the reader into the flawed world of Karen Stone, where Meg Bishop, her best and closest friend, warns the actress about the imminent dangers of liaisons with local "pretty young boys of the pimp or gigolo class" (*The Roman Spring of Mrs. Stone* 19), emphasizing the traps she might fall into if she continued her love affair with Paolo. Meg Bishop is an enigmatic character representing the novel's shifter. She is the emblem of the author, "a woman journalist who had written a series of books under the basic title of Meg Sees, all dealing with cataclysmic events in the modern world and ranging historically from the civil war in Spain to the present guerrilla fighting in Greece" (14). Ms. Bishop's function is to see and write what she sees from the position of the implied author. "[T]en years of association with brass hats and political bigwigs" turned Meg into an epicene figure that "had effaced any lingering traits of effeminacy in her voice and manner" (14). Meg's "booming, incisive voice" combined with her "alert, military bearing" in the "queenly mink coat that she wore, the pearls and the taffeta dinner gown underneath," give this character a "rather shockingly transvestite appearance, almost as though the burly commander of a gunboat had presented himself in the disguise of a wealthy clubwoman" (14). Tennessee Williams, as he wrote in his *Memoris* (147) and as Felicia Hardison Londré emphasiszed (21), often identified himself with the unusual female characters he was creating usually as the protagonists of his dramas. Although Meg is not the protagonist of the novel, she embodies all traits pointing to the Williamesque author-function because of her omniscient, writer-like qualities and sexually subversive character.

The second part of *The Roman Spring of Mrs. Stone* flashes back into the marriage of Karen and Tom Stone, a union "that was haunted by a mysterious loneliness" (70). This "had come very close to disaster because of a sexual coldness, amounting to aversion" on the part of Karen, and "a sexual awkwardness, amounting to impotence" (70) on the part of Tom. Nevertheless, "the pathos has succeeded where the desire had not," (67) allowing them to "discover what both really wanted, she an adult child and he a living and young and adorable mother" (68). The name of Karen's husband in the novel reflects a subtle choice alluding to the name of the author, Thomas (Tom) Lanier Williams, and also to the character of the poet-narrator in Williams's memory play, *The Glass Menagerie* (1944). Despite these obvious parallels, this character does not meet the role of the shifter, which remains assigned to Meg Bishop.

Mrs. Stone's public existence was nevertheless more active than her private life. Karen's acting career culminated in her role as Rosalind in William Shakespeare's *As You Like It* when she had an "incident in the dressing room" (70) with a young, successful actor who played the role of Orlando. The brief sexual encounter has allegorical value here: the Shakespearian-like pastoral comedy that took place offstage and ended with Karen's subsequent professional victory over her young partner in Toledo turns into an Italian urban irony in Rome ending painfully in Karen's last amorous drift. Karen Stone reflects an ambiguous and complex character as a result of the roles she plays onstage and off. In the limelight, Mr. Stone portrays multiple facets of sexuality ranging from that of Rosalind, a young woman, who cross-dresses into Ganymede (a gay icon) to that of Julia, the teenager *inamorata*. Both Rosalind and Juliet find true love unlike Karen Stone who does not encounter real love but merely wanders through relationships, events and places.

The last part of the book focuses on the protagonist's "drift," a repetitive pattern which evolves into the principal metaphor of the book. Karen Stone lived through her roles. She acted in "various parts" but was "never ever" (20) living her own life. She has not known true love; instead, she drifted among her various personas believing that the world itself was a real stage. After her career and marriage ended, she decided to stop the drift in 'Roma,' a location that encoded the Latin word for 'love,' a place which if read inversely means 'amor'. Disappointed by her paid companion, Karen Stone decides to test another May-December relationship with a mysterious young man, "the figure of the solitary watcher" (114) who followed her all the time. This "solitary figure," who "alone had not seemed to drift while she was helplessly drifting" (116) was a young man of exceptional beauty in rags living in dreadful poverty on the street under an Egyptian obelisk with cryptic pagan engravings patiently waiting "to receive a signal of some kind from the upper windows or terrace of an ancient Palazzo" (10). And Karen, after she was deceived by her Italian *marchetta*, was ready to give him this sign. Thus, the young American actor who played Orlando as well as Paolo di Leo, the fortune hunting parasite, were only *intermezzo* erotic figures that lead her towards the mysterious street urchin symbolizing the angel of death who stopped the drift.

Interestingly, the first film adaptation of *The Roman Spring of Mrs. Stone*—screenplay by Gavin Lambert and additional writing by Jan Read—was released a year before the American auteur theory (1962) was published. Nevertheless, José Quintero's adaptation can hardly be ranked among the auteur movies as far as what the director is concerned. As Murphy states, in the case of *A Streetcar Named Desire*, Elia Kazan's and Tennessee Williams's "struggle for ownership was there almost from the beginning of this collaboration" (198), whereas in the first adaptation of *The Roman Spring of Mrs. Stone* Quintero "desired nothing more than to create the most effective material expression of the playwright's text that was possible" (199) both on stage and in film. Williams had the final say over many issues in Quintero's production (both on stage with other productions as well as in this film adaptation). This weakened the auteur position of the director.

In the 1961 version of the novel, Karen Stone is played by Vivien Leigh, who previously portrayed Scarlett O'Hara, the Southern belle in *Gone with the Wind* (1939). Leigh also starred as Blanche DuBois in Elia Kazan's *A Streetcar Named Desire* (1951). She had, as Palmer writes, a successful production history in Hollywood and was a star with "complex and appealing resonances of meaning" (219). Drawing on her star persona, especially through her previous role in another Williams adaptation, Leigh "was picked to portray an aging and mentally unstable actress who forms a liaison with a handsome young gigolo" (219). This role seemed perfectly fit with the star's private life at the time of this production: she was a "successful actress whose fragile mental state and growing marital unhappiness" resulted in an "adulterous misadventure" which became a "sensational public knowledge" (219) at the beginning of the sixties in America. Consequently, Vivien Leigh became the key code that "linked the spectator's knowledge about the sexual transgression of film stars" (219) with the Williamesque topics of *The Roman Spring of Mrs. Stone*. She was the main extradiegetic transgressor who became the filmic shifter by 'importing' into this adaptation the image of a previous Williamesque emblem, Blanche DuBois. Similar to her earlier Southern belle characters, Leigh, as Karen Stone, confronted once again mainstream Hollywood heteronormativity with less visible facets of unmapped sexual desires.

Sexual transgression is encoded right from the first minute in Quintero's film: Karen cross-dresses as Ganymede and then she appears as the bride Rosalind. Meg Bishop played by Coral Browne appears from the beginning of the film, but unlike Meg in the novel where she is the obvious shifter of the author, here she remains a figure assigned to perform the role of a simple journalist-friend. Both in the novel and in the Quintero adaptation, Tom Stone is an asexual character. He is virtually absent from this movie version but one not devoid of power, as the rich man; however, good-looking Paolo (Warren Beatty) remains a plain companion and a sexual device for the financially powerful Mrs. Stone, who seems to be in a subordinate position while her marriage lasts, but relocates herself into a power position after her wealthy husband dies. Similar to the figure of Blanche in *A Streetcar Named Desire*, the explicit eroticism of Vivien Leigh's Mrs. Stone is toned down in the movie for censorship reasons and despite a half-hearted attempt to reveal her half-naked body; she appears far from being a sexual object. Instead, it is the male characters who reflect the all-pervasive sexual appeal in this movie.

The film's ending is foretold by a jealous Paolo through the story of a murdered wealthy woman from the French Riviera:

> A middle aged-woman was found in bed with her throat cut from ear to ear, almost decapitated. She was lying on the right side of the bed and there were stains of hair oil on the other pillow. No broken lock, no forced entrance. Obviously the murderer had been brought in by the lady and gone to bed with voluntarily! (Williams, *The Roman Spring of Mrs. Stone* 96)

This passage, taken verbatim from the original text of the novel, illustrates along with other numerous examples from the film that this adaptation was made primarily through the intersecting category where, as Dudley Andrew states, "the uniqueness of the original text is preserved to such an extent that it is intentionally left unassimilated in adaptation" (454).

Quintero's faithful film adaptation of the novel is at the level of the traditional *cinéma de papa*, which was characterized by a set of canonical works of literature faithfully script-led. Taken into consideration the Americanization of the auteur theory updated in the context of the post-structuralist auteurship, we can see that the auteur in the above case is not Quintero, the film's director. When directing this big screen movie, he could have made his name as auteur but failed to do so because he left many parts of the novel unmediated for the screen version. Quintero remained only a *metteur-en-scène* here.

The auteur function in this film adaptation is to be attributed to Vivien Leigh, the film star, whose intertextual presence has a powerful impact to produce another Leigh movie. The highly gifted Vivien Leigh in her role as Karen Stone successfully interweaves the role of the filmic shifter with that of the implied auteur. As the star of "this gloomy, pessimistic portrait of the artist as a middle-aged widow" (*Variety* 1961) and of the previously adapted play of Williams (*A Streetcar Named Desire*), Leigh brought into this new adaptation not only her own previous auteurial elements as a film star but also a number of Williamesque emblems with which she posits herself as the implied center who articulates the ideological voice of the filmic narrative and thus becomes the implied auteur of this film.

Robert Allan Ackerman's adaptation of the novel (with the writing credits of Martin Sherman) brings forward the previously neglected figure of Tom Stone (Brian Dennehey), and puts more emphasis on the male characters. After her poor performance as Juliet, Karen Stone (Helen Mirren) is visited by her husband, producer Tom Stone. Meg Bishop, the shifter of the novel, does not appear in this version of the novel. Instead, Ackerman's film cunningly devises a special character and assigns him the personal traits of the novel's author. This character is Christopher (Roger Allam), Karen's best friend, who bears a striking similarity to Tennessee Williams. According to Palmer and Bray this movie's script "was faulted for its insertion of a Tennessee Williams character whose presence" served, as the commentary wrote, as a "distraction rather than as a convincing persona" (291) in the intradiegetic world. On the contrary, this insertion greatly helped the permutation of the filmic shifter of the transgendered figure of Meg Bishop from the first version into that of the ghost-figure of the author himself. Similar to Williams, the gay character Chris (see Williams *Memoirs*, 145) writes plays for Karen and is always present when she is on and off-stage. He looks like Williams, speaks with a Southern drawl and comes to see Karen accompanied by Guido, a young man reminiscent of Williams's long-term Italian companion, Frank Merlo. Chris, as the alter ego of Williams, is thus, the film's shifter. The implied auteur of this version is also Christopher, the shifter and the filmic alter ego of Williams, who functions as the intradiegetic dramatic author.

Ackerman's version for television transforms Williams's novel to a greater degree than the previous version because the directory uses the most frequent mode of what Andrew calls borrowing and "employs, more or less extensively, the material, idea, or form of an earlier, generally successful text" (454). Nevertheless, Ackerman, like Quintero, falls under the spell of the novel and—ignoring the criteria of value from the American definition of the auteur—metaphorically 'hand over' the auteur function to the author of the novel in the absence of a film star, or screenwriter (see in this regard David Kippen's *Schreiben Theory: A Radical Rewrite of Film History* published in 2006) or any other individual with a special personal signature among the creative team. As a result, the 2003 adaptation of *The Roman Spring of Mrs. Stone* endows Tennessee Williams with the auteur function.

Below is a chart that sums up different functions in the novel and in the two consequent film adaptations:

	The novel	The 1961 adaptation	The 2003 adaptation
Author	T. Williams	Story: T. Williams	Story: T. Williams
		Screenplay: G. Lambert	Screenplay: M. Sherman
Director	-----	José Quintero	Robert A. Ackerman
Shifter	Meg Bishop	Vivien Leigh	Christopher
Implied author	Meg Bishop	-----	-----
Implied auteur	-----	Vivien Leigh	Christopher
Auteur function	-----	Vivien Leigh	T. Williams

In Tennessee Williams's novel both the shifter and the implied author is Meg Bishop, a minor epicene character. In José Quintero's film the shifter is embodied by the transgressive Vivien Leigh enacting Karen Stone, while the implied auteur and the auteur function are also accomplished by Leigh because she represents the transtextual cultural code referring to the figure of the novel's author in the absence of a director with strong personal style. Then, in Ackerman's television adaptation, both the shifter and the implied auteur are enacted by the gay playwright, Christopher, a minor character referring to the author of the novel, whereby the film's auteur is undoubtedly Tennessee Williams. This reflects an interesting setup of shifter, implied auteurship and auter function from the novel to each film version that conveys the unique style of Williams who authored the basic text complemented by the Leigh's star charisma that was inextricably bound with the hallmarks of William's works. While the big screen could accommodate a film star endowed with the auteur function, the TV version, despite Christopher's creative presence, was unable to go beyond a slightly altered *Auto-renfilm* label.

The two versions of *The Roman Spring of Mrs. Stone* rely heavily on the original novel with the same title. This narrative has a substantial cinematic potential, similar to Williams's successfully adapted plays, many of which developed out of his short stories. The name of the novel's author pervades both filmic discourses and generates though gender shifts and variable character correlations an ideological continuity that materializes in the complex forms of the implied auteur and auteur. Seymour Chatman observed that the study of relationships between film(s) and novel(s) reveal "with great clarity the peculiar powers of the two media" (436). The comparison between the two film versions of *The Roman Spring of Mrs. Stone* draws the attention to various types of negotiations in terms of the author function during the process of transformation. Williams recognized the effectiveness of different media to convey his world from the page to the stage and film, and he enthusiastically supported the adaptation of his stage successes to the realm of moving images. In doing so, as Palmer stressed, he provided the fifties' and sixties' Hollywood studios with literary material that created the Tennessee Williams film subgenre which transformed the American film industry (221, 231). Most of Williams's works have cinematic properties that can facilitate the transcendence of this unique voice from the literary medium into the filmic one and even from one film into the other. Ackerman's version owes much to Quintero's film and is viewed sometimes in the shadow of the former. One obvious example is Helen Mirren's striking resemblance to Vivien Leigh's Karen Stone, especially in term of her appearance (her dresses and her hair style). Leigh, the Williamesque transgressive shifter from the 1961 version, encoded the figure of the playwright; in the 2003 version, Christopher, as the obvious gay character alluding to the author of the novel came out of the closeted position. A similar gender shift occurred in the case of the implied auteur and also in the case of the auteur-function between Quintero's and Ackerman's version of *The Roman Spring of Mrs. Stone*.

Far from being a typical film auteur, Williams must be credited for initiating a revolution in taste and the transformation of the national character through the medium of the cinema, an important shift which, as Palmer concludes, "would have never have happened without the wholesale transference of his artistic vision from the stage to the commercial screen" (231). As a result, Tennessee Williams secured himself and his name a place not only in the American literary canon but also in the American auteur system.

Works Cited

Ackerman, Robert Allan, dir. (2003). *The Roman Spring of Mrs. Stone*. Showtime Networks. Writer: Martin Sherman, Story: Tennessee Williams. Producer: James Flynn, Cinematography: Ashley Rowe, Editing: Melissa Kent, Costume: Dona Granata, Music: John Altman, Cast: Helen Mirren, Brian Dennehey, Olivier Martinez, Anne Bancroft, Roger Allam, Rodrigo Santoro, Runtime: 108 minutes. DVD.

Andrew, Dudley. (1999). "Adaptation." *Film Theory and Criticism. Introductory Readings*. Fifth Edition. Eds. Leo Braudy and Marshall Cohen. Oxford: Oxford University Press, 452-460. Print.

Booth, Wayne. (1983). *The Rhetoric of Fiction*. Chicago: University of Chicago Press. Print.

---. (2002). "Is These an 'Implied' Author in Every Film?" *College Literature*, 29. 2 (Spring): 124-131. Print.

Chatman, Seymour. (1999). "What Novels Can Do That Films Can't (and Vice Versa)." *Film Theory and Criticism. Introductory Readings*. Fifth Edition. Eds. Leo Braudy and Marshall Cohen. Oxford: Oxford University Press, 435-451. Print.

Cook, Pam, ed. (1993). *The Cinema Book*. London: British Film Institute. Print.

Cristian, Réka M and Zoltán Dragon. (2008). *Encounters of the Filmic Kind. Guidebook to Film Theories*. Szeged: JATEPress. Print.

Hardison Londré, Felicia. (1983). *Tennessee Williams*. New York: F. Unger Pub Co. Print.

Hayward, Susan. (2003). *Cinema Studies: The Key Concepts*. London and New York: Routledge. Print.

Fries, Laura. (2003). "The Roman Spring of Mrs. Stone." *Variety*, May 1, 2003. Web. Retrieved from: http://www.variety.com/review/ VE1117920644?refCatId=32. Access: May 21, 2011.

Foucault, Michel. (1991). "What is an Author?" *Modern Criticism and Theory: A Reader*. Ed. David Lodge. London: Longman, 197-210. Print.

Murphy, Brenda. (1999). "Seeking Direction." *The Cambridge Companion to Tennessee Williams*. Ed. Matthew C. Roudané. Cambridge: Cambridge University Press, 189-203. Print.

Nánay, Bence. (2003). "Meghalt a szerző. Éljen a szerző!" ["The Author is Dead. Long Live the Author!"]. *Metropolis* 2003/4: 8-19. Print.

Palmer, R. Barton. (1999). "Hollywood in Crisis: Tennessee Williams and the Evolution of the Adult Film." *The Cambridge Companion to Tennessee Williams*. Ed. Matthew C. Roudané. Cambridge: Cambridge University Press, 204-231. Print.

Palmer, R. Barton and William Robert Bray. (2009). *Hollywood's Tennessee. The Williams Films and Postwar America*. Austin: University of Texas Press. Print.

Roudané. Matthew C. (1999). "Introduction." *The Cambridge Companion to Tennessee Williams*. Ed. Mattherw C. Roudané. Cambridge: Cambridge University Press, 1-10. Print.

Quintero, José, dir. (1961). *The Roman Spring of Mrs. Stone*. Production: A.A Productions, Seven Arts-Warner Bros., Producer: Louis de Rochemont, Writers: Gavin Lambert and Jan Read, Story: Tennessee Williams, Producer: Louis De Rochemont, Music: Richard Addinsell, Cinematography: Harry Waxman, Film editing: Ralph Kemplen, Costume design: Pierre Balmain and Beatrice Dawson, Cast: Vivien Leigh, Warren Beatty, Lotte Lenya, Coral Browne, Jeremy Spencer, Jill St. John. Runtime: 103 minutes. DVD.

Sarris, Andrew. (1999). "Notes on the Auteur Theory in 1962." *Film Theory and Criticism. Introductory Readings*. Fifth Edition. Eds. Leo Braudy and Marshall Cohen. Oxford: Oxford University Press, 515-518. Print.

"The Roman Spring of Mrs. Stone." (1961). *Variety*. Film Reviews, Sunday, December 31, 1961. Web. Retrieved from http://www.variety.com /review/VE1117794550?refcatid=31. Access: May 21, 2011.

Tinyanov, Jurij. (1981). *Az irodalmi tény*. Trans. Ágnes Réthy and András Soproni. Budapest: Gondolat. Print.

Williams, Tennessee. (1969). *The Roman Spring of Mrs. Stone*. Harmondsworth: Penguin. Print.

---. (1975). *Memoirs*. New York: Doubleday and Co, Inc. Print.

3. 1. 2. Who's Afraid of Adapting Albee?
Synergic Auteurship in *Who's Afraid of Virginia Woolf?*

I suspect that people who saw the movie *Who's Afraid of Virginia Woolf?* got
an approximation of the play, got some sense of what the play was about.
Edward Albee

The cinema is both a window and a mirror. The window looks out on the
real world both directly (documentation) and vicariously (adaptation).
Andrew Sarris

Mike Nichols's adaptation of Edward Albee's *Who's Afraid of Virginia Woolf?*
displays intricate questions pertaining to the issue of filmic authorship. Who
can claim the authorship over this film? Is it a matter of director versus
playwright? Are there additional participants competing for this function?
This chapter aims to reflect on these seemingly straightforward questions.

The film, its reception and the critical texts pertaining to it evince essential points connected to Andrew Sarris's Americanization of the *auteur* theory. In 1962 Sarris adapted the French *politique des auteurs* to American
filmmakers by outlining the three key premises of a genuine movie director:
first, the "technical competence" a film director must have when making a
film; second, the "distinguishable personality" of the director as an artist,
displayed in certain "recurrent characteristics of style" (Sarris 516); and
third, the "interior meaning" poetically described as "the ultimate glory of
the cinema as art" (516). The ambiguously formulated "interior meaning" is
a more complex concept that is "extrapolated from the tension between a
director's personality and his material" (516). This term encapsulates a concept that is "not quite the vision of the world a director projects nor quite
his attitude toward life" in an ambiguously intricate expression because

63

"part of it is imbedded in the stuff of the cinema" but "cannot be rendered in noncinematic terms" (516). François Truffaut has poetically called interior meaning "the temperature of the director on the set," a phrase that depicts only a metaphorical "approximation of its professional aspect" (qtd. in Sarris 516). Actually, Sarris's third premise involves not only the technical competence and the artistic talent of a director, but also a distictive "presence of spirit" including, as I wrote in *Encounters of the Filmic Kind*, a multitude of "communicative skills and other spontaneous attitudes a director needs to overcome" through "diverse obstacles during the entire process of filmmaking" (67) in order to have the film made and released. This third element is the most essential component 'assembling' the name of the cinematic author—the auteur.

Peter Wollen's work on the auteur theory shifted the focus from the three basic criteria of the auteur to a multiplicity of constitutive factors and emphasized that "any film," and especially "a Hollywood film, is a network of different statements, crossing and contradicting each other, elaborated into a 'coherent' version" that uncovers the most important layer providing the film with "energy cathexis" (532). This pooled assembly of energies was mostly associated with the name of the director-auteur because "it is through the force of his preoccupations that an unconscious, unintended meaning can be decoded in the film, usually to the surprise of the individual involved" (532). While this investment recalls the sum of skills that are the basis of Sarris's interior meaning, the cathected energies Wollen talks about point to an interactive effort rather than to a single individual. Subcribing partially to the structuralist approaches that focused on what Geoffrey Novell-Smith called the "core of basic and often recondite motifs" (qtd. in Wollen 521), Wollen believes that there is an unintended meaning, which can be and usually is assigned to an individual, but leaves open the question of team-work in filmmaking.

This chapter concentrates on the specific design of the interior meaning that shapes filmic auteurship in Mike Nichols's *Who's Afraid of Virginia Woolf?* produced by Warner Brothers Studios in 1966, which is an adaptation of Edward Albee's drama *Who's Afraid of Virginia Woolf* openning in 1962 at the Billy Rose Theater in New York. The play won the New York Drama Critics' Circle Award for best Play (1962-1963) as well as the Tony Award for Best Play (1963).

Movies are, according to Susan Hayward, "more marked by economic considerations" (5) and other protean factors than the literary work they adapt, regardless of the converted literary genre. These, usually extadiegetic complex components, have a strong "impact on the way the original text is interpreted" (5). Film is a system contingent upon various cultural, historical, social, political, and technological policies, in addition to other, interpersonal contexts. Film adaptations are, accordingly, "synergies between the desire for sameness and reproduction" containing "the acknowledgement of difference" (6). Since they are based on "elision and deliberate lack" adaptations favor "even to excess" certain "narrative elements or strategies over others" (6). At their onset, adaptations naïvely celebrated the writer of the book, the screenwriter (as in the case of *Autorenfilms* and in the *cinema de papa*) or the studio (company) as the sole author of the movies. Later, the director of the film became the quasi-romantic source of all significations and the name of canonized film directors amplified what André Bazin called "the aesthetic cult of personality" (qtd. in Wollen 520).

The controversies over authorship boiled down to disputes over the validity of individual contributions and 'signatures.' During the 1960s and at the beginning of the 1970s the Dziga Vertov Group lead by Jean-Luc Godard and Jean-Pierre Gorin claimed collective authorship and dismissed the personal element from the definition of a film's author. Robert Stam, following Pauline Kael, pointed out that film is a collaborative process standardized in "group style" (91) and ascribed important authorial roles to other persons of the movie's creative team. Films, as Linda Hutcheon emphasized, are "like operas" and give credit to "many and varied artists involved in the complex process of their creation" (825). Thus, as Richard Corliss remarks, "the real joy in movies" is the result of "the fortuitous communion of forces (story, script, direction, acting, lighting, editing, design, scoring)" (608) that contribute to the making of successful films.

If film is, as outlined above, an intertext of many factors, then authorship over this artifact can also be a network of individual contributions illuminating the cohesive activity of the filmmakers as team. Conceived as *synergic auteurship*, this creative team outperforms the function of the film director as sole auteur and is a more genuine marker of the filmic work of art. Taken into this context, Sarris's third criterion—the interior meaning—is a key concept that can open a critical space of alternative auteurship because it contains all the personal and extra-personal elements that can additionally help redefine the former, monolithic concept of filmic auteurship.

Despite the controversy stirred up by its profane content and perhaps due to the turmoil its topic and its use of language, *Who's Afraid of Virginia Woolf?* established Albee as an acclaimed American playwright, who brought into the thespian realm one of the most tabooed dramatic metaphors of his time: life after marriage. But Albee was not the sole artist to focus on the problematic issues within the American nuclear family and on precarious relationships between spouses at the beginning of the 1960s; subversive attitudes towards sexuality within and outside the domestic realm became apparent earlier with the publication of the *Sexual Behavior in the Human Male* (1948) and of the *Sexual Behavior in the Human Female* (1953) by Alfred Kinsey, two seminal works that triggered the proliferation of such topics in the of works of contemporary fiction writers. For instance, Richard Yates's novel *The Revolutionary Road* (1961) was published a year before *Who's Afraid of Virginia Woolf?* appeared on stage, while Betty Friedan's *The Feminine Mystique* (1963) came out a year after the production of Albee's drama. All tackled in various forms what Friedan called the "problem that has no name" (57) but it was only Albee's play that opened Pandora's box of secrets related to all members of the family.

The two main characters of *Who's Afraid of Virginia Woolf?*, Martha (Elizabeth Taylor) and George (Richard Burton), have been living on the academic campus of Nouveau Carthage, which was 'ruled' by Martha's father, the president of this small New England college. Their marriage has been marked by continuous verbal fights and language games of which they have become masters. As Enikő Bollobás pointed out, the most important game characters play in this drama is irony, with George and Martha as the "ironists" always present "with enough objectivity, disengagement, freedom, dispassion and critical attitude to perfectly fulfil this role" toward Nick (George Segal) and Honey (Sandy Dennis) as the "objects of irony" (325), whose "ignorance and involvement" is constantly changing (325). A newcomer colleague, Nick, and his wife, Honey, are invited, after a party, to visit George and Martha. This visit turns into a long-night drinking session of fun and games seasoned with true stories and painful discoveries on the part of each character, where the use and abuse of language is the main tool and weapon.

The first challenge the adaptation of the play faced was the conversion of a dense, witty and provoking dramatic text into a dynamic visual set-up that aimed to construct a (brave) new world on the basis of Albee's initial "Nouveau Carthage" setting involving the academic background and the domestic realm of George and Martha. The second main challenge was the choice of actors, while the third involved the mise-en-scène related to setting and photography. The use of a dense language of irony (the dialogues and the register of language) in this adaptation ended up in confronting American film censorship in a manner similar to that of *A Streetcar Named Desire* (1951, dir. Elia Kazan). As R. Barton Palmer writes, Kazan's adaptation became the first American adult film after winning the ideological battle with the Production Code Administration, then the major censoring institution in film industry (212-221). Despite the seminal changes *A Streetcar Named Desire* caused in the censoring policy of the fifties, Nichols's film managed to further provoke the Production Code Office in the sixties. The consequence was the overhauling of the Production Code Seal that passed or withheld the release of moving images (*Who's Afraid of Virginia Woolf?* Internet Movie Database) until 1965.

Geoffrey Shurlock, then head of Hollywood's Production Code Administration, refused to approve the release of *Who's Afraid of Virginia Woolf?* primarily because of its use of profane language, but he was eventually overruled by the Production Code Review Board, which stated that the film was, according to Mel Gussow, "not designed to be prurient" but was trying to be a faithful "reproduction" of an "award-winning (and thus already accepted) play" (241). After many hindrances, the film finally received the approval seal but the Production Code Review Board made it clear that the exemption they made with this movie did not mean that the "floodgates were open for language and other morally dangerous material" (241) for forthcoming movies. Nevertheles, despite this statement, the power of the censoring office decreased substantially: the institution had to review its restrictive policy and started to use a milder classification system of rating. Jack Valenti, who became the the the president of the Motion Picture Association of America (MPPA) in 1966, recalled the crisis that emerged from Nichols's adaptation, emphasizing the serious compromises that had to be made about the use of specific words and phrases. He said that

> [A]lmost within weeks in my new duties, I was confronted with controversy, neither amiable nor fixable. The first issue was the film "Who's Afraid of Virginia Woolf," in which, for the first time on the screen, the word "screw" and the phrase "hump the hostess" were heard. In company with the MPAA's general counsel, Louis Nizer, I met with Jack Warner, the legendary chieftain of Warner Bros., and his top aide, Ben Kalmenson. We talked for three hours, and the result was deletion of "screw" and retention of "hump the hostess," but I was uneasy over the meeting. ("How It All Began")

Who's Afraid of Virginia Woolf? by Edward Albee, with its "loud" and "vulgar" (94) characters, was among the first American dramas to use obscene, vulgar and expletive words, as, for instance, "bugger" (55) and "son of a bitch" (79); its film adaptation was among the first in that medium to use similar words along Rhett Butler's (Clark Gable) today classic sentence of "Frankly, my darling, I don't give a damn" in *Gone With the Wind* (1939, dir. Victor Fleming). Filmmakers had to either delete sections with profane words or to change them into milder forms. Expressions like "[S]crew you," "screwed up," and "personal screwing machine" from the initial text of the drama (21, 47, 92) and screenplay were replaced with "God damn you," and, as Tim Dirks writes, only after this conversion did the MPAA ratings board give the film a seal of approval releasing it with "[S]uggested for Mature Audiences" warning (see also *Who's Afraid of Virginia Woolf?* Internet Movie Database). The result was, as the Valenti document states, a new kind of "frank and open" production subject to "very few self-imposed restraints" ("How It All Began"), which was released as a result of a difficult confrontation. According to drama critic Stanley Kauffmann, this movie was "one of the most scathingly honest American films ever made" (qtd. in Gussow 241) and this was due to its use of ironic language games. Nichols's controversial movie, with its exorcized household matters and toned down adult dialogues, came out victorious on several fronts: not only did it lead to the demise of the Production Code and the establishment the film rating system but it also became a huge box-office success being the first film nominated for the Academy Awards in every eligible category. Furthermore, the film was even canonized: the adaptation of this 'notorious' play won five Oscars. Elizabeth Taylor received the Oscar for the Best Actress, Sandy Dennis for the Best Supporting Actress, Haskell Wexler gained the Academy Award for black-and-white cinematography, Irene Sharaff for Best Costume Design and Richard Sylbert for Best Art Direction.

During the adaptation of Albee's drama one of the most interesting conversions envisages the film script. The transposition of the play into a screenplay was a process that put Ernest Lehman, the film's producer and official screenplay writer of the movie, into a difficult position within the authorship test. Despite the fact that the film was advertised as "Ernest Lehman's production of Edward Albee's *Who's Afraid of Virginia Woolf?*" rather than a Mike Nichols film, as Gussow writes, "Lehman was the forgotten man" (242). According to Gussow, Albee stated that Lehman contributed only two lines to the movie, namely: "Let's go to the roadhouse" and "Let's come back from the roadhouse" (232). Nichols supported Albee's claim and insisted that all the other lines in the screenplay were Albee's (qtd. in Gussow 232). Later, Albee criticized Lehman again and said that the producer 'hired himself' to write the screenplay for $250,000.

The final screenplay was, in fact, an almost faithful replica of the play. When Mike Nichols, Richard Burton and Elizabeth Taylor read Lehman's script, they changed it back to Albee's original text with the exception of the two above-mentioned lines that ironically cost the production $125,000 a piece (see *Who's Afraid of Virginia Woolf?* Internet Movie Database). The playwright did not literally take part in the making of the movie but wrote Lehman a letter in which he made clear his claim over the authorship of the film text. Albee claimed that the film "was my play fucking word by word" (qtd. in Gussow 243), with a "few excisions" (242) that were unnecessary. Nevertheless, while acknowledging that the few additions Lehman made to the final film text concerning "phrases about going to and coming from a roadhouse" were quite helpful for the film version because they "broke the claustrophobia of the play" (242), Albee concluded the letter to Lehman ironically by writing he was "delighted" to see that "no rewriting had been done" and expressed his wish to compare the script with the play "some day" (242). In another interview, the playwright recalled the circumstances in which the play was transposed into film, shedding light on Hollywood's peculiar strategies of converting texts into movies by changing the most important issues contained in the original text:

And so the rehearsals started. They rehearsed for two weeks by using the play, which was very intelligent—as a stage play. Now, when plays are made into movies, there is a screenplay, and it's usually not written by the playwright. And this is meant to make the physical limitations of the play... you know, to 'open the play up,' so to speak. And it led to all sorts of things that made the play more like a movie. Now I realized it's a very "talking" play here. But I was fascinated by the reports I would get from Nichols: that the producer was writing; that the producer had hired himself, and was submitting screenplays, which nobody liked. This was getting in the way of getting production started. I'm told that in one of his many screenplays, the non-existent child had been changed into a deeply-retarded real child that was kept up in the attic. This convinces me that I'm right about the Hollywood mentality. (qtd. in Donovan 2006)

Lehman's own direction notes were indicating some cuts and changes, which were, in fact, only minor alterations of the original play but for which he ultimately received the screenplay credits. As Andre Soares observed, "[i]n the case of *Who's Afraid of Virginia Woolf?*, the most impressive film in Lehman's career, the screenwriter's job was akin to that of a book editor" who has not improved Albee's play, but only managed "to trim it without losing the author's original vision" (2005)—an activity that was far from real screenwriting. Even though "Lehman's editorial work was surely highly accomplished," Soares continued, *Who's Afraid of Virginia Woolf?* "owes its artistic success to the performances (thanks in large part to Nichols's solid handling of his actors), and to the characters and situations," which were Albee's, and not Lehman's creations (2005). And these performances were largely indebted to histrionic traditions that actors imported into the world of the film.

The history of cinema, as Susan Sontag pointed out, is generally seen as "the history of its emancipation from theatrical models" (362). Drama adaptations into movies advance "from theatrical stasis to cinematic fluidity" and from "theatrical artificiality to cinematic naturalness and immediacy" (362). On the one hand, theatre is "confined to a logical or continuous use of space;" on the other hand, cinema—through the editing process—"has access to an alogical or discontinuous use of space" (367). Albee's play takes place in virtually one room. Lehman made the shift from this static theatrical mode to cinematic fluidity by breaking the play out of its monotonously confined living-room space filled with an uncontrollable sentimentality and moved it into a dynamic setting consisting of various rooms; he also placed a few events outside the house thus adding an extra environment, the roadhouse—which turned out to be, as Kauffmann saw it, a "patently forced move" needed for the film's "visual variety" (1966), which finally turned less vital for the film's dynamism.

Lehman first rewrote the play on the basis of the criticism written about the Broadway performance of the play, which was, according to Gussow, centered around the idea of the imaginary child too seriously (236) and—perhaps in a willingness to conform to the expectations of critics and mainstream society or in his excessive wish to make an invisible character visible on the screen—he intended to make the fictional son of George and Martha a real character in the film. This character was to commit suicide "by hanging himself in a closet at the age of sixteen (his age would be lowered several years to make him a better match with Taylor as his mother)" (236). The idea of a real son was immediately rejected by the rest of the creative crew because a factual son would have undermined the ironic world of the couple and with it, the entire essence of the play. The other change Lehman wanted to implement in the movie script was a scene with two dogs fornicating at the beginning of the movie; this second attempt at freely rewriting the original text was also disregarded by the production team simply as irrelevant to the plot.

The only thing in which studio leader, Jack Warner, the director Mike Nichols and producer Ernest Lehman agreed was that the film should be made in black and white. The main reason behind this strategy, however, was not the fimmakers' wish that the movie appear more stylish or abstract but because, as Gussow pointed out, Taylor's heavy make-up was simply too harsh for a color version (236). Given these conditions, for Kauffmann it was obvious that a great part of "the real job of 'filmizing' was left to the director" (1966) and to the cinematographer rather than to the producer or screenplay writer. Albee saw this black-and-white production of his drama only as a minor alteration of the dramatic frame. The colorless version the playwright ironically called "Pastel Wexler" was in fact very close to the mood and the tone of the play and the lack of color did not take away any of the play's merits. Albee recalls his reaction to this situation in the following:

> I went to see a rough cut, before the music was put in. And then I was aware that something else was bothering me: I had written this play in color; I didn't write it in black-and-white. I mean, the characters up on stage looked like you guys, in color. I didn't put them in black suits and white makeup. It was in color. And the film was in black-and-white, even though oddly Pastel Wexler (?), the film photographer, said he had shot the film on color stock, and when it came to test it was in black-and-white. So it occurs to me that since he shot it on color stock, they might possibly someday have it made into a color version. I don't know. It's very unusual for a playwright to get the movie made of his play without long text changes. (qtd. in Donovan 2006)

The playwright was in the context of this moviemaking, as Gussow put it, "a kind of absentee landlord" (233), who officially had no say over the screenplay which, but which, ultimately, turned out to be his unaltered text, thus making him part of the synergic auteurship as the (sole) writer of the text. If the hallmark of the best screenwriters is, according to Corliss, "versatility" (610) then Albee can, in this sense also, be considered as the film's screenwriter. His text was more versatile than any of Lehman's versions. Additionally, Albee suggested Bette Davis and James Mason for the roles of Martha and George, respectively, but this proved to be an unsuccessful interference. Gussow recalls that Davis and Mason were both disregarded as possible actors for these roles by the producers and the studio alike (233), despite the fact that Davis played the role of Rosa Moline in *Beyond the Forest* (1949, dir. King Vidor) a film inserted as one of the intertextual references in Albee's drama.

Lehman, acting in his quasi-authorial function (less as screenplay writer and) mostly as a producer, "managed to get the difficult project off the ground" by "cutting large chunks of the play so as to keep the film's running time at a movie-audience friendly 130 minutes," Soares notes (2005). He had an important say at least over the cast because while most "[c]reative roles were played by the director, the actors, and the cinematographer," he was, as Gussow stated, the one who chose Elizabeth Taylor to play Martha (233). Taylor was considered by most members of the creative crew a doubtful choice because she seemed too young for the role of 52-yeal-old Martha, suggested, together with costar Richard Burton, a "fresh, young director" fit for a "young play" (qtd. in Gussow 234) about middle aged characters. Despite the fact that *Who's Afraid of Virginia Woolf?* was to be Mike Nichols's first film, after a series of successful Broadway directions he was finally appointed by the studio as the movie's director because Burton and Taylor, as Gussow explains, then at the height of their popularity, cornered the creative team and told them that they would either have Nichols to direct the film or else—similar to the fun and games of George and Martha in Albee's play—they would "eat" any other director alive (234). Their threat was taken seriously because, as Kevin Hagopian commented, Taylor's and Burton's star power and charisma, their "on-screen chemistry" coupled with the "complete domination of the nation's gossip columns with their endless romantic shenanigans" had increased spectators' appetites "for more Taylor-Burton films" ("Film Notes. *Who's Afraid of Virginia Woolf?*"). This production could not afford to lose its film stars and so, despite Jack Warner's initial reluctancy to hire him, Nichols was appointed as a director chosen by its actors to guide their performance.

According to Leo Braudy, besides performing "a role as he creates a kind of life, playing between his characterization in a particular film and his potential escape from that character, outside the film and perhaps into other films" (421), a film actor needs to have a more powerful personality than that of a stage actor. Movie actors have to "draw upon the resources of personality much more than stage actors do" because film actors "can never do anything out of character" which is made obvious through their presence on screen (421). Thus, as Hutcheon remarks, many actors are actual "adaptors of screenplays" (82). Taylor and Burton belong to this type of actors-stars. For Robert C. Allen, the concept of stardom involves the duality between actor and character, between the on-screen persona and the off-screen person (547) or, as Christine Gledhill termed it, the "reel" character and the "real" (qtd. in Hayward 352) person. Taylor and Burton both created an intradiegetic and an extradiegetic star-world, each combining their "reel" and "real" figure into that of a star figure, who intertextualized the name of the actor from film to film—occasionally the other's name, too, especially in movies in which they co-starred—thus making their way into the realm of joint authorship.

Taylor became a star in the fifties and sixties. She played—among many other films—in two Tennessee Williams adaptations, *Cat on a Hot Tin Roof* (1958, dir. Richard Brooks) and *Suddenly Last Summer* (1959, dir. Joseph L. Mankiewitz) and in *Cleopatra* (1963, dir. Joseph L. Mankiewitz). Burton has made a name in Hollywood with *Cleopatra* (in which he costarred with Taylor) and *The Night of the Iguana* (1964, dir. John Houston), another famous Tennessee Williams adaptation. In many cases, as Corliss stresses, actors who are stars turn out to be the auteurs of the movie(s) in which they play (608). On the basis of their previous movies, the Taylor-Burton duo's fortuitous collaboration elevated them from the star-as-person status to star-as-text level, assuming that the former influenced the latter (Dyer 626). Hence, Burton and Taylor teamed with Nichols as star-auteurs of the *Who's Afraid of Virginia Woolf?* became part of the synergic authorship team.

The plot line of *Who's Afraid of Virginia Woolf?* was slightly altered from the original text. So were the film's characters. For Bazin, actors in a movie create "a whole new mythology existing outside of the original text" (qtd. in Hayward 4) because of the interaction between their on-screen and off-screen personality. Albee's *dramatis personae* entail, as I write in "Edward Albee's Castings, "a construction specific to the name of the playwright," a careful composition of roles and a "special rendering of the characters" (135) that are converted in the film version by the actors' artistic vision combined with their star auras. Stage characters are mostly archetypal, whereas in the movies one demands special individualization that suggests a greater power to the figures on the screen (Sontag 366). Taylor, for example, became the "author" of her own character because s he was allowed to create her own Martha on the screen.

Referring to Taylor's memoir, Gussow mentions that the actress had never seen Albee's play onstage before playing in the movie; she even refused to listen to the original cast recording because she wanted to create a character of her own that was not confined to any previous Martha models (238). As a result, Taylor's on-screen persona turned out to be a "desperate woman" with the "softness of the underbelly of a baby turtle" that she covered up with the "toughness of the shell" which she painted red, so the figure appears "sloppy," "slouchy" and "snarly" (238)—an accurate image the actress had at that time in the media. Dwight Garner noticed that there was "something wildly entertaining about watching Taylor and Burton, two actors at the top of their craft, wickedly knock the crap out of each other" (1997) in this ironic movie about marriage games. Their stardom auras enlisted them almost automatically along with Nichols (whom they choose) and Albee (whose adapted text was almost verbatim the orginal play) as partner auteurs of this film. Patrick McGilligan suggested that the issue of the director-auteur be revised and rethought with actors in mind because

> under certain circumstances, an actor may influence a film as much as a writer, director or producer; some actors are more influential than the others; and there are certain rare few performers whose acting capabilities and screen personas are so powerful that they embody and define the very essence of their films. If an actor is responsible only for acting but it is not involved in any of the artistic decisions of film-making, then it is accurate surely to refer to the actor as semi-passive icon, a symbol that is manipulated by writers and directors. But actors who not only influence artistic decisions (casting, writing, directing, etc.) but demand certain limitations on the basis of their screen personas, may justly be regarded as 'auteurs.' (qtd. in Dyer 625)

While praising the film's director, Taylor emphasized that Nichols was an ingenious person, who "had the actors participating in his inventions" (qtd. in Gussow 239), thus acknowledging her share of synergic authorship in the process of making *Who's Afraid of Virginia Woolf?*. Likewise, partner in this synergic auteurism, Burton attributed a central role to Nichols as "author" of the film and credited him with "certain ruthlessness" (qtd. in Gussow 239) while directing the movie. Nichols accepted actors' suggestions and even conspired with them in order to get the best scenes. In the end, the director achieved exactly what he wanted but this did not take away from the artistic merits of the actors-auteurs.

Nichols—along with Stanley Kubrick, Richard Lester and Norman Jewinson—was once dismissed by Sarris in *American Cinema* as "a director whose work was less than meets the eye" (qtd. in Hill 2003). Nevertheless, Nichols's two great films that "insured his A-list status among filmmakers," *Who's Afraid Of Virginia Woolf?* (1966) and *The Graduate* (1967), showed that the young but experienced stage director turned into film director "utilized all the toys available" to become an auteur name in Hollywood right his first film. He employed, as Lee Hill puts it, "self-conscious editing and cinematography, stylized production design, hypernaturalistic acting" and had "a willingness to break down the crumbling dictates of the Hays Code" (2003). Moreover, as Kauffman noted, Nichols had a peculiar artistic vision and special

> skills of keeping the camera close, indecently prying; giving us a sense of his characters' very breath, bad breath, held breath; tracking a face - in the rhythm of the scene - as the actor moves, to take us to other faces; punctuating with sudden withdrawal to give us a brief, almost dispassionate respite; then plunging us in close again to one or two faces, for lots of pores and bile. (Kauffmann 1966)

According to Hill, he personified the "European ideal of the personal filmmaker" (2003) and with the above-mentioned qualities managed to fit the first two criteria for the American auteur (technical competence and personal style), as outlined by Sarris a couple of years before Nichols directed his first film success. The director's technical knowledge, as Mark Estrin points out, materialized in "foreground shooting, long takes, and distorting close-ups" and was aimed "to intensify the sense of his characters' entrapment"; he often employed in his films the "overlapping sound and a spare, modernistic mise-en-scène (the latter at times reminiscent of [Michelangelo] Antonioni) to convey an aura of disorientation and sterility" (see "Mike Nichols") that provided the signature of the director as artist.

Who's Afraid of Virginia Woolf? was, as Hill mentions, simply "a pitch-perfect translation of Albee's absurdist play" (2003). Moreover, Kauffmann observed that "[a]ny transference of a good play to film is a battle" (1966) that is generally avoided even by the best film directors. When a director adapts a successful play, Kauffmann continues, it is increasingly difficult to struggle against leaving the drama's "natural habitat;" this was the case of Albee's "extraordinary comedy-drama" that managed to set "a stiff fight" for the young director of the film (1966). Nichols, teamed with Taylor and Burton, demonstrated not only the director's "genius for translating theatre to film" (1966) but also the creative power of the entire artistic crew behind the official name of the film director. Nichols credited the teamwork process and acknowledged that the major difference between directing a play and a film lie in what Gavin Smith termed as "couching" (1999) the creative team behind the movie.

What he described here as "couching" was an important element of the third criteria of the auteur, interior meaning. The 'mystery' that stands behind the director's ability to translate a written text into the filmic realm involves instructing a team of artists, technicians and managers and make this team work in specific situations and environments. Despite the fact that he was a wise trainer, there is no indication that Nichols ascribed the film to himself; instead, he recognized the synergic authorial function of virtually every creative member of the filmmaking, with special regard to Edward Albee.

Any coherent notion of auteurism today, as Stam emphasizes, should take into account the "diverse intrications in terms of material circumstances and personnel" (90). This is best described by what Stam calls the "invisible narration" (91) of the film creators. This "invisible narration" of *Who's Afraid of Virginia Woolf?* is 'told' by a synergic auteurship construction consisting of Mike Nichols (director), Richard Burton (George), Elizabeth Taylor (Martha), and Edward Albee (playwright). Nichols put special emphasis on the credits Albee had in this production by declaring that the movie "it's so much a play" in which "people sit around a living room and talk" but which "doesn't seem like a play" (qtd. in Gussow 243). The director added that this is "more Edward's accomplishment" (243) than his own artwork and admitted that the success of adapting Albee's complex play on screen was due to the fact that he has always felt "a vague, unreasonable kinship" with the playwright, with whom he had felt "connected in some way" (qtd. in Gussow 20).

Who's Afraid of Virginia Woolf? was in Gussow's view "astonishingly successful at transferring the play into another medium" (244). A close comparison of Albee's play to the film version can open up what Zoltán Dragon described as "a space for intertextual dialogue" where the two texts start to reveal "hidden aspects of themselves for each other" as well as for the interpreter (30, 31). In case of Nichols' work the film adaptation points at "specific interpretative possibilities" of Albee's play, while the dramatic text 'talks about' the movie by highlighting the nature of transposition (Geoffrey Wagner) rather than that of the analogy (Dudley Andrew) that is established between the two texts.

The dialogue in the film was trimmed down, as Gussow observed, "to bring the running time down" (244) but in all other important respects, even Gussow recognized that the movie "faithfully captures the brilliance" (244) of Albee's play by almost faithfully recycling its world. For Smith, one of the decisive factors for a fortunate translation of dramatic text to film is the story that has to be contained in both (1966). Some stories seem to be able to undergo an accurate reproduction that can ultimately "convey" the original text but "can't stand the pressure of the process or confrontation by the audience" and therefore "certain metaphors" might "crack under that pressure" (1966). Albee's text supplemented by Nichols's vision, in the context of synergic auteurism, managed to stand this confrontational pressure and brought into moving pictures a hidden domestic story about a euphemism that reflected social and even political anxieties of the period and which contributed to the movie's artistic and box office success. This success centered on the signifying power of the fictive son, the central metaphor that was the engine of the movie.

Who's Afraid of Virginia Woolf? cannot claim a unique auteur; instead it has a synergic auteur function by paying, as Gussow writes, "credit to all parties," beginning with Albee and including "Nichols, and the actors" (245). Lehman and Warner, the invisible managerial crew has nevertheless to be acknowledged at least "for not interfering with the essence of the material" (245). Generally, the Hollywood studio background in filmmaking was, according to Thomas Schatz, "less a process of collaboration than of negotiation and struggle—occasionally approaching armed conflict" (606). But, as Schatz indicated, "somehow it worked, and it worked well" (606). So was in the case of *Who's Afraid of Virginia Woolf?*. A cultural product of the turbulent sixties, this movie was more than a film. It was, in Kauffmann's words, a "notable event" (1966) in American film history leading to the elimination of the Production Code in 1967 and to the introduction of the MPAA film rating system in 1968; however, its most important merit was that it challenged the rigid notion of auteurship right from the emergence of the Americanization of auteur theory.

Works Cited

Albee, E. (1965). *Who's Afraid of Virginia Woolf?* Harmondsworth: Penguin. Print.
Allen, Robert C. (1999). "The Role of the Star in Film Industry" (From *Film History: Theory and Practice*). *Film Theory and Criticism. Introductory Readings*. Fifth Edition. Eds. Leo Braudy and Marshall Cohen. New York: Oxford University Press, 547-561. Print.
Bazin, André. (1999). "Theater and Cinema" (From *What is Cinema?*). *Film Theory and Criticism. Introductory Readings*. Fifth Edition. Eds. Leo Braudy and Marshall Cohen. New York: Oxford University Press, 375-386. Print.
Bollobás, Enikő. (1981). "Who's Afraid of Irony? An Analysis of Uncooperative Behavior in Edward Albee's *Who's Afraid of Virginia Woolf?*" *Journal of Pragmatics. An Interdisciplinary Quarterly of Language Studies* 5: 323-334. Print.
Braudy, Leo. (1999). "Acting: Stage vs. Screen (From *The World in a Frame*)." *Film Theory and Criticism. Introductory Readings*. Fifth Edition. Eds. Leo Braudy and Marshall Cohen. New York: Oxford University Press, 419-425. Print.
Corliss, Richard. (1992). "The Hollywood Screenwriter." *Film Theory and Criticism. Introductory Readings*. Fourth Edition. Eds. Gerald Mast, Marshall Cohen and Leo Braudy. New York: Oxford University Press, 606-613. Print.
Cristian, Réka M. (2002). "Edward Albee's Castings." *Eger Journal of American Studies. Vol. VIII.* Ed. Lehel Vadon, Eger: Eszterházi Károly College, 135-170. Print.

---. (2008). "Cinema and Its Discontents: Auteur, Studio, Star." *Encounters of the Filmic Kind. Guidebook to Film Theories.* Cristian Réka M. and Dragon Zoltán. Szeged: JATEPress, 63-81. Print.

Dirks, Tim. "Who's Afraid of Virginia Woolf?," *Filmsite Movie Review.* Web. Retrieved from: http://www.filmsite.org/whos.html. Access: March 31, 2008.

Donovan, Aine. (2006). "Transcript of Edward Albee Lecture/Q&A") Darthmouth College, April 26, 2006. Web. Retrieved from: http://www.dartmouth.edu/~ethics/docs/newsletter_2006winter.pdf and http://209.85.135.104/search?q=cache:mPrjYGV_TwQJ:www.dartmouth.edu /~ethics/announce/documents/AlbeeLecturetranscribed.doc+%22who%27s +afraid+of+virginia+woolf%22%2B%22mike+nichols%22&hl=hu&ct=clnk& cd=315&gl=hu&client=firefox-a. Access: February 22, 2008.

Dragon, Zoltán. (2008). "Do You Speak Film? Film Language and Adaptation." *Encounters of the Filmic Kind. Guidebook to Film Theories.* Cristian Réka M. and Dragon Zoltán. Szeged: JATEPress, 21-33. Print.

Dyer, Richard. (1992). "From *Stars.*" *Film Theory and Criticism. Introductory Readings.* Fourth Edition. Eds. Gerald Mast, Marshall Cohen and Leo Braudy. New York: Oxford University Press, 622-627. Print.

Estrin, Mark W. (updated by H. Wayne Schuth, further updated by Robyn Karney). "Mike Nichols." Web. Retrieved from: http://www.filmreference.com/Directors-Mi-Pe/Nichols-Mike.html. Access: March 17, 2008.

Fleming, Victor, dir. (1939). *Gone With the Wind.* Selznick International Productions, Producer: David O. Selznick, Screenplay: Sidney Howard, Writer: Margaret Mitchell, Cineamtography: Ernst Haller, Music: Max Steiner, Distributor: Metro-Godlwyn-Mayer and Warner Bros, Cast: Clark Gable, Vivien Leigh, Leslie Howard, Olivia de Havilland, Hattie Mcdaniel, Butterfly McQueen. Language: English, Runtime: 224 minutes. DVD.

Friedan, Betty. (2001). *The Feminine Mystique.* New York: W.W. Norton and Company. Print.

Garner, Dwight. (1997). "Who's Afraid of Virginia Woolf?" (March 21, 1997). Web. Retrieved from: http://www1.salon.com/march97/garner970321.html. Access: February 20, 2008.

Gussow, Mel. (1999). *Edward Albee: A Singular Journey. A Biography.* London: Oberon Books. Print.

Hagopian, Kevin. "Film Notes. *Who's Afraid of Virginia Woolf?*" Web. Retrieved from: http://www.albany.edu/writers-inst/webpages4/filmnotes/ fnf01n2.html. Access: February 25, 2008.

Hayward, Susan. (2003). *Cinema Studies. The Key Concepts* (Second Edition). New York: Routledge. Print.

Hill, Lee. (2003). *Mike Nichols.* Web. Retrieved from: http://www.sensesofcinema.com/2003/great-directors/nichols. (June 2003). Access: March 11, 2008.

Hutcheon, Linda. (2006). *A Theory of Adaptation.* New York and London: Routledge. Print.

Kauffmann, Stanley. (1966). "Film Notes. *Who's Afraid of Virginia Woolf?*" (from *The New York Times*, June 30, 1966). Web. Retrieved from:

http://www.albany.edu/writers-inst/webpages4/filmnotes/fnf01n2.html. Access: February 25, 2008.

Nichols, Mike, dir. (1966). *Who's Afraid of Virginia Woolf?* Warner Bros. Pictures, Producer and Screenplay: Ernest Lehman, Story by: Edward Albee, Cast: Elizabeth Taylor, Richard Burton, George Segal, Sandy Dennis, Music: Alex North, Cinematography: Haskel Wexler, Language: English, Runtime: 131 minutes. DVD.

Palmer, R. Barton. (1999). "Hollywood in Crisis: Tennessee Williams and the Evolution of the Adult Film." *The Cambridge Companion to Tennessee Williams.* Ed. Matthew C. Roudané. Cambridge: Cambridge University Press, 204-231. Print.

Sarris, Andrew. (1999). "Notes on the Auteur Theory in 1962." *Film Theory and Criticism. Introductory Readings.* Fifth Edition. Eds. Leo Braudy and Marshall Cohen. New York: Oxford University Press, 515-518. Print.

Schatz, Thomas. (1999). "The Whole Equation of Pictures. (From *The Genius of the System*)." *Film Theory and Criticism. Introductory Readings.* Fifth Edition. Eds. Leo Braudy and Marshall Cohen. New York: Oxford University Press, 602-606. Print.

Smith, Gavin. (1999). "Mike Nichols - Noted filmmaker - Interview." *Film Comment.* (May 1999). Web. Retrieved from: http://filmcomment.net/fcm/5-6-99/mnintrgs.htm. Access: March 18, 2008.

Soares, Andre. (2005). "Ernest Lehman." (Posted: July 6, 2005.). *Alternative Film Guide. Thinking Film.* Web. Retrieved from: http://www.altfg.com/blog/classics/ernest-lehman. Access: March 3, 2008.

Sontag, Susan. (1992). "Film and Theatre." *Film Theory and Criticism. Introductory Readings*, Fourth Edition. Eds. Gerald Mast, Marshall Cohen and Leo Braudy. New York: Oxford University Press, 362-374. Print.

Stam, Robert. (2000). *Film Theory. An Introduction.* Malden, Mass.: Blackwell. Print.

Who's Afraid of Virginia Woolf? From *Internet Movie Database.* Web. Retrieved from: http://www.imdb.com/title/tt0061184/trivia. Access: February 22, 2008.

Valenti, Jack. "How It All Began." Web. Retrieved from: http://www.mpaa.org/Ratings_HowItAllBegan.asp. Access: March 1, 2009.

Vidor, King, dir. (1949). *Beyond the Forest.* Warner Bros. Pictures, Producer: Henry Blanke, Screenplay: Lenore J. Coffee, Written: Stuart D. Engstrand, Cast: Bette Davis, Joseph Cotton, Music: Max Steiner, Cinematography: Robert Burks, Language: English Runtime: 97 minutes. DVD.

Wollen, Peter. (1999). "The Auteur Theory. (From *Signs and Meaning in Cinema*)." *Film Theory and Criticism. Introductory Readings.* Fifth Edition. Eds. Leo Braudy and Marshall Cohen. New York: Oxford University Press, 519-535. Print.

Yates, Richard. (2008). *The Revolutionary Road.* New York: Knopf Doubleday. Print.

3. 2. Negotiation, Characters, and Identity

The second section of the "Sites of Identity Through Cinematic Vistas" part is "Negotiation, Characters and Identity," which contains an essay on the identity construction of the protagonist in Julie Taymor's *Frida* and a transnational map of identities in the making as shown by a number of characters in Alejandro González Iñárritu's film, *Babel*.

"Negotiating Identity in Julie Taymor's *Frida*" is a commentary of Frida Kahlo's intricate sites of identity, as they appear in the American women director's film. This visual narrative discloses the identity of the Mexican artist as a person belonging to an array of discursive traditions, which in Taymor's visual narrative appears as negotiated identity that shifts between sexualities, between the private and political body, between conventional and unconventional life, amid ability and disability, among different art forms (photography and painting), languages (Spanish and English), and cultures (Tehuana and European, Mexican and American). The "pleasurable negotiation" of the film is achieved through the strategies of classical narrative cinema fused with an original scheme subverting stereotypical representation of women.

"Transnational Negotiations in Alejandro González Iñárritu's *Babel*" is a study on a series of attitudes and identities at play that condition curious transnational negotiations with global impact between the main characters of *Babel*, both "Middle-Worlders" and cosmopolitans. The first depicts the identity of the the individuals constructing specific bridges between cultures in a tense and sometimes adverse political climate; the latter defines the ideal conditions of the relationships between and among individuals on the cross-cultural arena. The negotiations in this movie fall between these two categories and result in a visual narrative placed in specific contact zones, where characters test the(ir) limits of language and culture: in the Moroccan desert and at the windows of the tourist bus, at the Tijuana border crossing and through the telephone interface, on the family balcony of the elegant middle-class apartment in Tokyo, and on the television screen through which media relates the seemingly unrelated events, which turn out to be intimately connected.

3. 2. 1. Negotiating Identity in Julie Taymor's *Frida*

Ahí les dejo mi retrato/
pa' que me tengan presente [...]
Here I leave my portrait/
so that you'll remember me [...]
Frida Kahlo

Julie Taymor's film entitled *Frida* (2002) contributed immensely to the worldwide phenomenon known as 'Fridamania' that was ignited by the popularity of Frida Kahlo's art works promoted by Neomexicanismo and feminist movements of the 1980s. Kahlo (1907-1954), the legendary self-taught Mexican painter of mixed ancestry, became a cult figure by the 1990s. Kahlo joined the ranks of other famous women painters—Artemisia Gentileschi, Georgia O'Keefe, Tamara de Lempicka, Leonora Carrington, Amrita Sher-Gil (also nicknamed the Indian Frida Kahlo)—all of whom excelled in the art of visual representation by illuminating subtle facets of their individual identities. Taymor adapted the figure of Frida Kahlo played by Salma Hayek into a stylish performance and transposed her paintings into moving images fused with animated scenes by transferring Kahlo's visual identity to the big screen.

Frida Kahlo's mother, Matilde Calderón y Gonzáles, was a mestiza of Spanish and native Mexican descent. Her father, Guillermo Kahlo, was the son of Hungarian Jews from Arad, who moved to Germany where their son was born; later, Guillermo emigrated to Mexico and became, as stated in Hayden Herrera's biography of Kahlo, "the first official photographer of Mexico's cultural patrimony" (5-6, 7). He bought The Blue House in Coyoacán, Mexico City that became Frida's home and what Raquel Tibos saw as Frida's "personal kingdom" (8), where she found comfort and inspiration. Frida painted most of her paintings in this house, today a museum displaying a number of her art works. Her canvases are continuously featured in countless museum exhibitions as well as in virtual presentations and sell at record auction prices; concomitantly, her life continues to be the subject of various cultural commetaries.

Likewise, Julie Taymor's biopic pays homage to the multifaceted Kahlo in its cultural commentary interweaving the artist's subjectivity and art which reveal Kahlo's intricate sites of identity. Frida's identity profile is presented through the "aestheticized body" of her paintings disclosing a person who "speaks to an array of intersecting discursive traditions" that belong to an array of what Micki Nyman described as "national, postcolonial, feminist, Marxist, postmodernist, (bi)sexual, surrealist, and magical realist" (2010) contexts. The protagonist of *Frida* embodies the inner reality of emotions which materialize in eccentric visual representations by disclosing an unusual perception of love coupled with bodily pain. The private Kahlo appears consequently in a number of naïve, surrealist forms through which Frida, the artist, finds a way of expressing and negotiating her identity, a quest adapted by Taymor, too. Gregory Dechant, the translator of Kahlo's letters and texts, emphasized in the "Translator's Note" of *Frida by Frida* the fact that Kahlo's unique identity and her artistic expression was also akin to her mundane communication which reflected "a medium for that difficult conquest of liberty and self-realization to which she dedicated her life" (9).

Taymor's *Frida* is for Rex Reed an interpretive framework about these intricate discourses of liberation and fulfillment encompassing everything "from masterpiece to pure kitsch" (2002) in Kahlo's diegetic life. In this movie her art is presented sophisticatedly "prankish as its subject" (2002), while the artist's flamboyant style provides an unusual way of manifesting identity. Kahlo exposes her identity through intricate love processes in a film that is an outstanding example of contemporary negotiated cinema. Generally, negotiated films take into consideration the basic elements of classical visual narratives by fusing the visual pleasure these movies provide—as criticized by Laura Mulvey—with the subversive practices of alternative filmmaking into a pleasurable negotiaton of a special counter-cinema that represents revised cultural assumptions resulting in a new type of character I termed in *Encounters of the Filmic Kind*, the negotiated cinematic character (96). In Taymor's film, pleasurable negotiation is achieved through the strategies of classical narrative cinema fused with an original scheme subverting stereotypical representation of women. On the level of the classical narrative, this film is the love story of Frida and her husband Diego Rivera—played by Alfredo Molina—a classic romance embodying considerable subversive potential especially in terms of gender issues. The most important counterhegemonic element in this visual discourse is the alternative display of the woman artist through her own self-portraits. Taymor imports into the cinematic narrative Frida's art works representing the painter as seen by Kahlo herself. The projection of the protagonist's own works in the film, obviously part of a self-reflexive representational strategy, is a crucial element undermining the schemes of classical narrative cinema and pleasurable narratives that exhibit the woman as a sexualized object of scrutiny. To stress this strategy, the film's narrative focuses on the crucial moments of the artist's diegetic life that converge into Kahlo's paintings that are cloned into the film as moving images. These 'edited' images turn into facsimiles of Kahlo's painted canvases while the protagonist becomes, as mentioned in the "Gender and Cinema" chapter of *Encounters of the Filmic Kind*, a negotiated cinematic character and the model for an alternative cinematic practice of the woman's self-representation (96-97).

Frida is a personal history revised through Kahlo's paintings culminating in a gendered account of an idiosynchratic art history. In 1925, Gertrude Stein advocated the individualization of historical narratives with the first publication of *The Making of Americans*, an unconventional mode of evaluating the history of a nation imagined as an assembly of vernacular texts resembling verbatim transcripts of imagined oral histories that depicted individual and family narratives. Stein's experimental work foresaw a predilection for personal histories which developed into what Wes Gehring described as the "penchant for biography" on national inclination level, especially during the last decades, when "the American public has been especially drawn to the chronicling of lives" (2003) through various media by adapting history to personal modes of narration. By adhering to this tendency, Taymor reinterprets the traditional portraits of the artist and affirms a novel view on Kahlo's life and work by juxtaposing the layers of history's grand narratives with the unconventional stories of Frida's visual and written documents. Many of Kahlo's paintings display crucial moments of her identity quest contexualized in a regional American crisis of representation that occured in great part during the worldwide economic uncertainty culminating in the Great Depression. In this all-arching perspective Frida was similar to many Americans in the 1930s who, as Jonathan Veitch wrote, "found themselves in a world that was altogether different from the one into which they had been born" (5).

Apart form the larger economic and political circumstances of the first decades of the twentieth centruy, Kahlo found herself in a completely different world after she had a serious accident. Confined to bed, she began using visual metaphors to express the pain of her distressed body. According to Nicholas Mirzoeff, the body in visual art representations appears not as itself, but as a sign representing "both itself and a range of metaphorical meanings, which the artist cannot fully control, but only seeks to limit by the use of context, framing, and style" (3). Kahlo's paintings in the film, depict Frida's bodyscape of explicit signs, comprising a natural body, where the physical, "mutable, incomplete and altogether human" (2) figure is combined with Kahlo's body politic reflecting gender-conscious representation of her own body battles.

In a Public Broadcast Service interview with Bill Moyers, Taymor talked candidly about a couple of relevant points in her cinematic portrait of Kahlo. The film director emphasized the difference between Frida's image in the 1980s, when the figure of the Mexican woman artist "was used as an icon of pain and suffering," and the way this film aims to re-present her as "a woman who was outrageous, unique, talented, single minded, tenacious" and, above all, "very feminine." According to Taymor, Frida was "very much caught up with her man" and "very obsessive about her love" towards Rivera. Consequently, the film balanced this powerful passion by emphasizing the figure of a rather feminine and even domestic Frida who "knew how to lay a table" and "how to put flowers in her hair" with an idiosynchratic mystery which lay in "her gender bending, her bisexuality, her ability to be both macabre, grotesque and exquisitely beautiful, sublimely beautiful" (qtd. in "Bill Moyers" 2002).

These features depict Frida's negotiated identity, the result of a multitude of subtle negotiations between Kahlo as a radical artist and activist, and Frida as an exquisite woman represented by her artistic bodies displaying her multiple identities through a myriad of images and through various film techniques (such as the setup of dialogues, the use of special language use, Frida's clothing), which appear in a refined cinematic performance of femininity in Taymor's version of the artist's life. The director uses an array of nonliterary materials (photographs, paintings, sketches, clothes, jewelry, interior design, songs) besides a number of literary works (letters, a biography) in her adaptation of Kahlo's life. These elements, Julie Sanders explains, "enjoy an allusive intertexual relationship" (152) resulting in a special type of adaptation that employs a number of less unconventional parts. These, can be combined in what Peter Brooker calls a peculiar "pastiche" that has "something to do with differences in media and modes of production and reception" informed by certain "habits of cultural value," which are brought together in order to "re-function" (108) a (life) narrative 'imported' in this film0 from a conventional biography. Based on these materials, *Frida* falls rather into the category of postliterary adaptation than that of the literary adaptation. According to Thomas Leitch, postliterary adaptations are based on elements that have neither the full "cachet of literature nor the armature of a single narrative plot that might seem to make them natural Hollywood material" (258). Moreover, this film is based on a large number of historically accurate data, making this film a work "based on a true story" that "appeals to the authority of a master text that has all the authority of a precursor novel or play or story" but "with none of their drawbacks" (289)—another important postliterary feature.

Similar to the real Frida Kahlo, Taymor's Frida does not claim one distinct identity: she exhibits a range of Fridas which present the identity of the artist within the frames of a classical narrative system by engaging in various encounters that highlight her subjective facets as daughter, as woman, as lover, as wife, as artist, as friend, as modernist, as Mexican, as patient, as political activist.

Frida's intricate relations in film are patterned by an uncanny figure mediating her identity. This enigmatic figure is Guillermo Kahlo acted by Roger Rees in Taymor's film. The deeply affectionate parent-child relationship between Frida and her father was of crucial importance, especially in Kahlo's art. Despite its obvious importance, Taymor's filmic narrative minimizes this paternal presence and focuses more on Kahlo's complex relationship with Rivera, who becomes thus a metaphorical father surrogate. The film recognized this transfer and Frida's indirect acknowledgment of this shift. Kahlo, as her letters testify, was very conscious of labeling her relationship with Rivera and usually avoided calling Diego her "husband" because, as she wrote in her "Portrait of Diego,"

> that would be ridiculous; Diego has never been, not will he ever be, anyone's "husband." Nor as my lover for he embraces much beyond sexual limitations, and if I spoke of him as of a child, I would only describe or paint my own emotion, almost my self-portrait, not that of Diego. (qtd. in Tibol 344)

She spoke of Rivera by the telling and showing of her own truth "in order to trace an outline," within her powers, "of his image" (qtd. in Tibol 344). Taymor's movie conforms to the usual romantic story and does not elaborate on Frida's relationship with her father or on Rivera's position as father figure. Instead, the movie replaces this powerful image with a number of emblematic alternatives, objects and episode rather than deliniating clearly this presence.

This movie also presents the protagonist's patient-doctor encounters of parentification and dependence only briefly despite the fact that Frida left a considerable number of letters and paintings related to the physicians she was treated by throughout her life. These texts and artifacts document Frida's filial affection towards her doctors which materialized in subtle processes of sentiment transference. During these processes the figure of her father is inextricably linked with the figure of her physicians. By paying Frida's surgeons and specialists, Guillermo assisted his daughter's healing. Additionally, he gave her a canvas on which she could start painting while she was confined to bed after the tram crash when her spinal column was fractured.

Guillermo's work inspired his daughter to create her own photographs and later, her paintings. Both father and daughter were attracted by the power of visual representation; Guillermo earned his living from it while Frida used it first as therapy and later as a tool of self-expresion. Bedridden for a period of time, Frida observed her motionless body in a mirror hanging above her bed and then started to paint the plaster of her body cast with her father's watercolors and oils, making herself the model of a self-appointed art. Her father also brought her useful tools and canvases on which Frida painted her first works. Her craft originates in her love of photographic art. Similar to the size of photos, as the Herrera biography shows, most of her paintings are relatively small, and their scale is adapted to "the intimacy of their subject matter" (xii), which is, in most cases, a portrait. With Guillermo's encouragement, Frida starts painting while she is immobilized in bed. Her father's photographic laboratory is symbolically transformed into the daughter's (bed)room of her own art. Painting links Frida to her father's artistic practice, which she sublimates into a unique heritage of visual representation. Later, Frida marries Diego Rivera, painter and muralist, whom she meets by way of her art. On a symbolic level, Frida develops her father's mechanically reproduced art into a visual art form of her own, which emerged as an outcome of the accident that changed her life.

Taymor's film focuses on the surreal representation of a streetcar crash as the crucial point in Frida's art. While trying to grasp the gold powder offered by a delivery boy on the tram, the protagonist of the movie is caught in a Max Ernst-like vision, in which she moves across some visual thresholds connecting the moving images of the film. Kahlo's perception of this event is depicted by her in two emblematic paintings entitled *Accidente [The Accident]* (1926) and in *El camión [The bus]* (1929). After the crash, Taymor's Frida denies close contact with men, with the exception of her father and her doctors. She is very conscious of everything she says afterwards and even makes up a story about her first sexual encounter informing her doctors that she lost her virginity during the accident when a metal shaft perforated her abdomen. With this explanation Kahlo transposes her sexual life into a medical event by transferring her affective drives from 'unworthy' young men—depicted in the movie by her former lover, Alejandro Gómez Arias (played by Diego Luna)—to those specialists who cure her. Back home in her baldachin bed, Kahlo confesses to her father that she feels as a girl waiting for her gentlemen callers, except that she is a patient and the callers are doctors.

This is an explicit case of what Sigmund Freud called transference love. Transference love is a mode of compensation by a substitute for love in which the patient's distressing ideas are associated with and transferred to the figure of the physician, in Joseph Breuer's and Sigmund Freud's term, as a "mésalliance" or "false connection" ("The Psychotherapy of Hysteria" 389-390). The transference in the case of a sympathetic doctor is called positive transference and usually happens when apparent personal relations are involved and the third person coincides with the figure of the physician (391). This third person in Taymor's film is Frida's father, and later, her husband, Diego. Prior to meeting the hedonistic Rivera, Frida witnesses a love affair between the artist and one of his models. The symbolic setup of this scene is similar to the Freudian primal scene in which the child witnesses its parents during the act of lovemaking. According to Freud, the child perceives this encounter as an aggressive act toward the body of the mother ("The Dream and the Primal Scene" 270). In Taymor's film, the young Frida witnesses the amorous moment from the position of the Freudian child, and also sees the disappointment and pain of Diego's first wife, Lupe Marin, who discovers the adulterous liaison. This moment will influence her relationship with Diego, who later becomes her husband.

During her troubled marriage with Rivera, Frida often transferred her sentiments to the doctors who have treated her. In the "Introductory Lectures on Psychoanalysis," Freud explains the cirmcumstances concerning the process of transference of the patient's feelings towards the person of the doctor by emphasizing that the readiness for a sentimental exchange of this kind derives from a preexisting affection. Transference, in this sense

> can appear as a passionate demand for love or in more moderate forms; in place of a wish to be loved, a wish can emerge between a girl and an old man to be received as a favorite daughter; the libidinal desire can be toned down into a proposal for an inseparable, but ideally non-sensual friendship. Some [...] succeed in sublimating the transference and in moulding it till it achieves a kind of viability; others must express it in this crude, original, and for the most part, impossible form. But at the bottom it is always the same, and never allows its origins from the same source to be mistaken. ("Transference," 494)

The series of medical treatments displaces the classical analytic treatment in this configuration of transference and offers Frida a renewed opportunity to dislocate her feelings of appreciation and gratitude from her father towards her first lover, Alex, then towards Diego and towards her doctors, some of whom ultimately become her close friends. For example, in a letter written to Dr. Leo Eloesser on July 23, 1935, Kahlo writes:

> I love you more than my own skin, and though you don't love me the same way, in any case you love me somewhat, no? Or if that's not true, I'll always have the hope that it may be, and that is enough for me... Love me just a little. I adore you. Frida. (qtd. in Tibol 158)

For Marco Casonato transference is "a metaphorical concept," operating as "a form of displacement" (2009). This continuos displacement of transference love plots Frida's life and especially her art. Although counter-transference or reenactment on the part of the doctor(s) as such did not happen (or were not documented), Dr. Eloesser became the life-long friend of the family, considered by the artist as the *par excellence* "doctorcito," who healed her real and metaphorical wounds, and on whom she could always count.

In Taymor's film, the transference love between Frida and her doctors is represented through a couple of episodes with no Kahlo paintings attached to them. Although Frida paints the portraits of almost all her doctors, the film does not emphasize the visual aspect concerning this transference love. However, in the extadiegetic world, the "Portrait of Dr. Leo Eloesser" painted in 1931 as a gift to Dr. Eloesser bears the inscription "Los Tres Amigos" [Three Friends], alluding to the three sails of a ship in the background of the picture, which represents the three characters participating in the process of transference love: Frida Kahlo, Leo Eloesser and Diego Rivera. In the light of Freud's descriptions of transference love, this particular process is "an emotional cathexis" that is transposed from an important person (Guillermo and Diego) onto the doctor, who was in reality indifferent to her, "so that the doctor will have been chosen as a deputy or surrogate for someone much closer" reminiscent of her father or husband whom she discovered in Eloesser ("Attempts at Interpretation" 181-182). According to Andrea Kettenman's biography, Frida dedicates—as her sign of affection and gratitude—another painting to Dr. Eloesser entitled *Autoretrato dedicado al Dr. Eloesser* [Self Portrait Dedicated to Dr. Eloesser] (1940) on which she writes: "Pinte mi retrato en año 1940 para el Doctor Leo Eloesser, mi medico y mi mejor amigo. Con todo mi cariño, Frida Kahlo" [Self-portrait dedicated to Dr. Leo Eloesser, my doctor and my best friend. With all my love, Frida Kahlo] (59). Later, she dedicates one to Dr. Juan Farill, which bears the title *Autoretrato con el retrato del Dr. Farrill/Autoretrato con el Dr. Farrill* [Self-portrait with the portrait of Dr. Farrill or Self-portrait with Dr. Farrill] (1951). In this painting, intended as a gift to Dr. Farrill and also featured in Kettenman's book (80), Kahlo sits in a wheelchair painting the portrait of her healer with her heart extended as the painter's palette and her blood as coloring device, all visual metaphors of an obvious process of transference love.

In "The Art of Being Patient," Servando Ortoll and Annette B. Ramirez de Arellano reflected on Kahlo's possible Münchausen syndrome by shedding light on a number of overexaggerated psychosomatic symptoms especially in the artist's eccentric relation with her doctors that lead to constant involvement in medical treatments coupled with intense physical dependency on the physicians who cured her. As a consequence, Ortoll and Ramirez de Arellano claim that Frida practiced a "double alchemy" by painting her body in art works with which she paid her healers (2004). This double alchemy was also part of the intricate process of transference love.

Guillermo Kahlo appears in Taymor's movie as a cryptic character that makes cameo appearances. His film profile is analogous to his portrait from Kahlo's canvas; the latter is a textual and visual tribute Frida paid to her father the same year she painted Dr. Farrill. At the bottom of this painting she wrote a phrase involving the name of her father, suggesting that he was both the implied artist and the object of her visual artform:

> I painted my father Wilhem Kahlo, of German-Hungarian origin, a photographer artist by profession, intelligent and refined, of a generous character, a brave man because he suffered from epilepsy for sixty years but never ceased to work and he struggled against Hitler. With adoration, his daughter Frida Kahlo. (qtd. in Tibol 363)

Kahlo's cinematic encounters in *Frida* include several forms of sublimated transference, some of which are also encoded into her art of painted stories. After she recovers, Frida decides to take her paintings to "Señior Rivera" for an artistic evaluation. On her way to Rivera, Frida's left hand holds her *pain*ting and her right hand the crutch. This image suggests that the combination of Frida the person, the artist, and the subject of her extended self in her painting negotiate her identity right from the beginning of the film. With her swollen leg, she is similar to a determined feminine Oedipus going straight ahead to face the Sphinx-like Rivera, whom she manages to surprise, outwit and delight with her painting and bright personality. Frida starts her first artistic endeavor by first showing her "Self-portrait with Velvet Gown" (painted in 1926 and actually given as a gift to Alejandro Gómez Arias, her first love). This sensual painting, which appears in the Kettenman volume, displays her Modigliani image focusing on her long Parmigianino neck (7) with aristocratic features that capture Rivera's mind, eye and, eventually, his heart. The natural, physical body of the artist becomes Frida's body politic through which she enters the public arena of the male dominated visual arts.

Kahlo in the film described her marriage with Rivera laconically as her "second accident" (*Frida*). The first accident produced lifelong bodily pains; the second was the source of other types of traumas in Kahlo's life. In Herrera's biography of Frida Kahlo, Diego is depicted as her "lover", "husband", "father", "child", who, from time to time, turns into Frida's "me." This tendency to identify occasionally with the sometimes paternal figure of Rivera in Taymor's visual narrative, appears at the beginning of their marriage when Diego and Frida appear as isomorphic bodies modeled after Kahlo's painting titled *"Frida and Diego or Frieda Kahlo and Diego Rivera"* (1931). Furthermore, in the atmosphere of the chic intellectual left at the party preceeding their wedding, Frida behaves as if she were an *alter ego* of Diego: to everyone's astonishment she drinks all men under the table and invites the attractive Tina Modotti (Ashley Judd) to dance a sexually charged tango with her. The dance turns out to be a good exercise in the construction of her identity. Following this episode, the film focuses on the domestic realm of the couple, where Frida 'dances' even more passionate 'tangos' than the one with Modotti, especially when she meets Rivera's former wife, Lupe Marín (played by Valeria Golino), in their kitchen right after the wedding. After an emotional outburst, Frida becomes an everyday participant in Lupe's kitchen and the two women, much to Diego's amazement, eventually become close friends and allies.

Taymor's Frida is a complex person with a sophisticated identity un-veiled especially through her love affairs with men and women of different ages and cultures. In the film, her miscarriages and her divorce from Rivera expose another face of Kahlo—the *Frida dolorosa* depicted "como el chile verde… picante" (*Frida*) culminating in the double self-portrait of *Two Fridas* (1939). Here the twin Fridas are connected by a blood vessel that highlights the haunting symbolism of the paternal figure: the European counterpart dressed in white linked to her father's heritage is slowly dying from blood loss, whereas the Mexican Tehuana alluding to her mother's heritage holds the hand of the other Frida. In her other hand a tiny talisman depicts a young Diego, as an uncanny male presence. This small icon is perhaps one of the most expressive imprints of Frida's shifting identity in terms of father figures validated by Kahlo's surrealist symbolism and by Taymor's narrative. As Diego's self-proclaimed "ancient concealer" (qtd. in Tibol 292), Frida conceals him not only in her letters but in her paintings as well. Another sublimated image of the Kahlo-Rivera visual isomorphism in Taymor's film is *Self- Portrait with Cropped Hair* (1940). The movie displays this episode of emblematic configuration by transposing Frida's post-divorce distress onto pictures: the artist cuts her long hair and wears her former husband's oversized clothes in a process of mourning. Taymor's Kahlo creates at this point in the movie a new identity, which resembles the boyish image of a *young paloma negra* from her father's 1926 family photo alluding to the prototypes of strong *indigenas* from northern Oaxaca and Sierrra Norte de Puebla, which are emphasized in the Kettenmann biography of the painter (55).

Taymor's *Frida* ends with the protagonist's art displayed in Mexico. Terminally ill, Kahlo insists to be taken on her bed to see her first Mexican exhibition. An exquisitely attired body on display on her bed as well as the subject of the canvasses she painted, Frida becomes part of the diegetic art show. Her pillow reads: *"Duerme Amor"* [*Sleep Love*], suggesting the closure of the transference-love process, where death is the ultimate object of love. With surrealistic paintings and live mariachis in the background, death comes to save this concealer. Taymor's movie is a continuation of this art show patterned by pain and lived through by various transferences: a close-to-complete portrait of the artist herself. "Magician and surgeon compare to painter and cameraman," Walter Benjamin writes in "The Work of Art in the Age of Mechanical Reproduction," and underlines that whereas the "painter maintains in his work a natural distance from reality, the cameraman penetrates deeply into its web" (675) of signification. Taymor is a magician in the Benjaminian sense and her ability to put together diegetic and non-diegetic facets of personality into a truly negotiated film creates a new type of movie which *profiles* multiple facets of identity not only through Kahlo's art but through the life of the artist combined with her own work of art, especially via Kahlo's self-portraits. The figure of the enigmatic father is a blindspot that conveys a distinguished cult value and a specific aura for this film. According to Benjamin, this cult value, which is inherent in photography and in painted portraits,

> does not give way without resistance. It retires into an ultimate retrenchment: the human countenance. It is no accident that the portrait was the focal point of early photography. The cult of remembrance of loved ones, absent or dead, offers a last refuge for the cult value of the picture. For the last time the aura emanates from the early photographs in the fleeting expression of a human face. This is what constitutes their melancholy, incomparable beauty. (670)

This beauty and melancholy of Guillermo Kahlo's photographs was further developed by Frida Kahlo in her own portraits in which she delineates a distinct site of negotiated identity also within the diegetic space of the film. Taymor's close-ups of Kahlo's painted portraits and filmic faces makes, as Béla Balázs writes, the hidden life of little things visible (260) in a visual anthropomorphism which uncovers the complex setups of transference love. *Frida* is a sensual testimony which enables an array of discursive practices about complex identities and about the way transference operates. Frida's negotiated identity is successfully presented in Taymor's film through the convergence of several discourses instead of focusing on one specific aspect of otherness because Kahlo's art, in Nyman's opinion, was the outcome of "such an array of discursive traditions" (2010). Kahlo's artistically counterhegemonic body influenced Taymor to create a negotiated identity for Frida Kahlo, whose fluid identity shifts between sexualities, between the private and political body, between conventional and unconventional life, amid ability and disability, among different art forms (photography and painting), languages (Spanish and English), and cultures (Tehuana and European, Mexican and American).

Works Cited

Balázs, Béla. (1992). "The Close-up. From *Theory of the Film*." In *Film Theory and Criticism. Introductory Readings*. Fourth Edition. Eds. Gerald Mast, Marshall Cohen and Leo Braudy. New York: Oxford University Press, 260-267. Print.

Benjamin, Walter. (1992). "The Work of Art in the Age of Mechanical Reproduction." In *Film Theory and Criticism. Introductory Readings*. Fourth Edition. Eds. Gerald Mast, Marshall Cohen and Leo Braudy. New York: Oxford University Press, 665-681. Print.

"Bill Moyers Interviews Julie Taymor." (2002). *Public Broadcasting Service*. November 29, 2002. Web. Retrieved from: http://www.pbs.org/now/ transcript/transcript_taymor.html. Access: May 23, 2011.

Breuer, Joseph and Sigmund Freud. (1991). "The Psychotherapy of Hysteria." Trans. James and Alix Strachey. Sigmund Freud and Joseph Breuer. *The Penguin Freud Library, Vol. 3., Studies on Hysteria*, Eds. James and Alix Strachey. Harmondsworth: Penguin, 388-393. Print.

Brooker, Peter. (2008). "Postmodern Adaptation: Pastiche, Intertextuality and Refunctioning." *The Cambridge Companion to Literature on Screen*. Eds. Deborah Cartmell and Imelda Whelehan. Cambridge: Cambridge University Press, 107-120. Print.

Casonato, Marco. (2009). "Transference: Love, Journeys, and Psychoanalysis." *PSYART: A Hyperlink Journal for Psychological Study of Arts*. December 15, 2009. Web. Retrieved from: http://www.psyartjournal.com /article/show/casonato-metaphor_and_psychoanalysis_transference. Access: May 10, 2011.

Cristian, Réka M. (2008). "Gender and Cinema: All Sides of the Camera." *Encounters of the Filmic Kind: Guidebook to Film Theories*. Réka M. Cristian and Zoltán Dragon. Szeged: JATEPress, 83-104. Print.

Freud, Sigmund. (1991). "Transference." Trans. James Strachey. *The Penguin Freud Library, Introductory Lectures on Psychoanalysis, Vol. 1.*, Eds. James Strachey and Angela Richards., Harmondsworth: Penguin, 482-500. Print.

---. (1991). "Attempts at Interpretation." Trans. James Strachey. *The Penguin Freud Library, Vol. 9. Case Histories II. The 'Rat Man,' Screber, The 'Wolf Man,' A Case of Female Homosexuality*. Ed. Angela Richards, Harmondsworth: Penguin, 168-195. Print.

---. (1991). "The Dream and the Primal Scene." Trans. James Strachey. In *The Penguin Freud Library, Vol. 9., Case Histories II. The 'Rat Man,' Screber, The 'Wolf Man,' A Case of Female Homosexuality*. Ed. Angela Richards. Harmondsworth: Penguin, 259-280. Print.

Gehring, Wes. (2003). "Reassembling the Dust: The Art of Biography - Reel World - Great Interest in Chronicling of Lives." *USA Today (Society for the Advancement of Education)*, March 2003. Web. Retrieved from: http://findarticles.com/p/articles/mi_m1272/is_2694_131/ai_98829814/. Access: May 16, 2011.

Herrera, Hayden. (2002). *Frida. A Biography of Frida Kahlo*. New York: Perrennial-HarperCollins. Print.

Kettenmann, Andrea. (2003). *Kahlo. Fájdalom és szenvedély.* [*Kahlo. Pain and Passion*] Trans. Magda Molnár, Budapest: Taschen/Vince. Print.

Leitch, Thomas. (2007). *Film Adaptation and Its Discontents. From Gone With the Wind to the Passion of the Christ.* Baltimore: The Johns Hopkins University Press. Print.

Mirzhoeff, Nicholas. (1995). *Bodyscape. Art, Modernity and The Ideal Figure.* New York: Routledge. Print.

Nyman, Micki. (2010). "The Disabled Body in Julie Taymor's *Frida.*" *Disability Studies Quarterly.* Vol. 30, Nr. ¾. Web. Retrieved from: http://www.dsqsds.org/article/view/1274/1304. Access: May 26, 2011.

Ramírez de Arellano, Anette B. and Servando Ortoll. (2004) . "Egy betegség művészete" [*The Art of Being Patient*] Trans. Réka M. Cristian. *Filmkultúra*, 2004. Web. Retrieved from: http://www.filmkultura.hu/regi/ 2004/articles/essays/ortoll.hu.html. Access: June 2, 2011.

Reed, Rex. (2002). "Frida: A Lush, Sensuous Trimph." *The New York Observer.* October 27, 2002. Web. Retrieved from: http://www.observer.com/ node/46651. Access: June 6, 2011.

Sanders, Julie. (2006). *Adaptation and Appropriation.* London: Routledge. Print.

Taymor, Julie, dir. (2002) *Frida.* Writer: Hayden Herrera, Screenwriters: Rodrigo Garcia, Clancy Sigal, Diane Lake, Gregory Nava, Anna Thomas, Edward Norton, Producer: Salma Hayek, Sarah Green, Jay Polstein, Lizz Speed, Nancy Hardin, Lindsay Flickinger, Roberto Sneider, Music: Elliott Goldenthal, Director of photography: Rodrigo Pieto. Costume designer: Julie Weiss, Makeup: John E. Jackson, Beatrice De Alba, Cast: Salma Hayek, Alfred Molina, Geofrey Rush, Mia Maestro, Roger Rees, Ashley Judd, Antonio Banderas, Edward Norton. Production: Handprint Entertainment, Lions Gate Films, Miramax Films, Ventanarosa Productions, Runtime: 123 minutes. DVD.

Tibol, Raquel, ed. (2006) *Frida by Frida.* Second Edition. Selection of Letters and Texts. Mexico City: Editorial RM. Print.

Veitch, Jonathan. (1997). *American Superrealism. Nathanael West and the Politics of Representation in the 1930s,* Madison: The University of Wisconsin Press. Print.

3. 2. 2. Transnational Negotiations in Alejandro González Iñárritu's *Babel*

> The global village is a place of very arduous
> interfaces and very abrasive situations.
> *Marshall McLuhan*

September 11, 2001 initiated a global crisis of trust that still seems to pervade many contemporary narratives. In *The Khazar Tournament–Against Contemporary Relativism* (published in 1997), Paul Cornea foresaw this crisis when he observed that one can effectively refute current sophism only by going beyond a rigid belief system in order to adopt trust as an alternative to "faith," which "separates" and "opposes" (10) us. In turn, Cornea continues, trust—willingly or unwillingly—"brings us together" and "unites" (10) people by finding, through various practices, the realm of collective humanity. The contemporary crisis of trust, which materialized predominantly in the war on terrorism, was reconfigured by diverse forms of post-9/11 rhetoric throughout the globe, with special regard to visual narratives produced in or outside the United States of America. This crisis has since had its visible or less observable symptoms in all areas of life, producing intriguing epitomes in times that Lidia Vianu aptly called our "desperado age" (2006).

Apart from this crisis, nevertheless still related to this particular moment, contemporary theories and methods in American studies tend to embrace—among many other approaches—comparative studies, critical internationalism, cosmopolitanism, and Postcolonial Studies. As Barbara Brinson Curiel, David Kazanjian, Katherine Kinney, Steven Mailloux, Jay Mechling, John Carlos Rowe, George Sánchez, Shelley Streeby, and Henry Yu argued in the "Introduction" to *Post-Nationalist American Studies*, this complex turn is concerned with "how one negotiates among local, national, and global perspectives, while remaining vigilantly self-critical about the episte-mologically and historically deep ties" that this field "has had to U.S. impe-rialism" (7). As Jane C. Desmond and Virginia R. Dominguez previously argued, a genuine internationalization of American studies needs an in-creased involvement of transnational exchanges, which, in turn, favor the creation and use of "new paradigms of research" under the aegis of cosmo-politan discourses (qtd. in Rowe 7).

In the following, I propose to survey the ways trust works through the specter of various characters which challenge transnational negotiations in an inherently transnational medium: film. Alejandro González Iñárritu's international co-production *Babel* (2006) is perhaps the best example of trust and its variant, the crisis of trust that appears in interpersonal relations in the contact zones of some specific parts of the world. As its title sug-gests, *Babel* alludes not only to the Biblical place where the confusion of languages took place (the Babylonian Babel, the Tower of Babel) but also to the very fact of language confusion and miscommunication ('babel of voic-es') that it induced. The movie's plot is shaped after this original confusion into a nonlinear narrative split into various scenes, eventually assembling a topography of miscommunications in a collage of identity mosaics that de-pict, as Terrence Rafferty noted, both the difficulty and the necessity of interaction (2006) and the ways in which people of diverse cultural back-grounds learn to relate to each other('s cultures) in critical contexts around the globe.

A Moroccan incident between the locals and tourists triggers a series of events reaching the United States of America, Mexico and Japan, and be-comes the source of a film that embodies a peculiar butterfly effect process. The concept of the butterfly effect, borrowed from chaos theory, is a meta-phor that describes the sensitive cause-effect dependence: any infinitesimal change can indirectly be related to a very remote object or being, for exam-ple, the flapping butterfly wings are able to ultimately cause significant changes (a hurricane, for example) on a large, even global scale. *Babel* sub-scribes to the butterfly effect plot line and transposes it into a transnational medium which exhibits intricate international exchanges that—activated at a local point—spreads globally.

The butterfly effect is a complex concept embodying the potential for static existence as well as the capacity for change. In his Metaphysics of Quality theory, Robert Pirsig coined two similar notions: one as the old, complex "static pattern" and the other, the "Dynamic Quality," which is "the source of all things, completely simple and always new" (57). For ex-ample, "[A] home in suburban Short Hills, New Jersey, on an ordinary Wednesday afternoon is filled with static patterns," (58) writes the author of *Lila: An Inquiry Into Morals* and continues by enumerating the facts behind static situations and those leading to the Dynamic Quality. Pirsig observes that a "hurricane in Key Largo promises a Dynamic relief from static patterns," while the "man who suffers a heart attack and is taken off the train at New Rochelle has had all his static patterns shattered" (58). Because the man "can't find them," he realizes that "in that moment only Dynamic Quality is available to him," Pirsig continues, emphasizing that the man "gazes at his own hand with a sense of wonder and delight" (58) because he has recognized the potential of change that the Dynamic Quality (i.e. the unpredicted, sudden change of his previous situation) holds in itself. While static patterns freeze the paradigms of structural systems (as for example, the belief systems or trust), the Dynamic of Quality provides the "quality of freedom" (59) that is endowed with an "increase in versatility" (72) which produces, among other effects, miscommunication and the crises of trust.

González Iñárritu's film is a visible metaphor of a number of obvious static patterns that appear in the four countries in which the film is set—Morocco, Japan, Mexico and the United States of America—and provides the narrative frame for the Dynamic Quality materialized in transnational exchanges which occur after a specific butterfly effect is set into motion. This analysis of *Babel* will, in addition to the previous notions of trust, crisis, static pattern and Dynamic Quality, be also assisted by the concepts of Breyten Breytenbach's "Middle World" and John Ryder's interpretation of cosmopolitanism.

The Middle World, according to Breytenbach, is not the Global Village but rather a symbolic space of encounter that is "equidistant from East and West, North and South;" it appears equally "belonging and not belonging" but exists mostly off the Center, and is, above all a "peripheral" (136) terrain. This locus seems to be a subtle derivation of the geopolitical notions of the First, Second, and Third Worlds and might refer to some features of the Fourth World. The Fourth World, as discussed in the chapter on "Third Cinema Encounters" in *Encounters of the Filmic Kind*, is a term with which Western thinking describes the status of peoples without states such as the Roma in Europe, Native Americans, Aboriginal Peoples or First Nations (sic) in North America and aboriginals in Australia, Tibetans in China (Tibet), and so on (107). Besides the political connotation which connects it to the Fourth World, the Middle World for Breytenbach has a complementary dimension that is "aware of the moral implication of the narrative" (152) its inhabitants produce. Most of these narratives are unconventional histories of the marginalized people, of the excluded, of the refugees and the exiles. "Because of their indefinable character," Maria Todorova writes in *Imagining the Balkans*, "persons or phenomena in transitional states, like marginal ones, are considered dangerous, both being in danger themselves," but also "emanating danger to others" (17), this danger being intimately connected with the concept of the crisis of trust in given contexts.

The residents of the Middle World are the so-called *Middle-Worlders*—people with a specific nomadic thinking who, in Breytenbach's definition, "promote diversity, sometimes by default" (139). Despite the fact that they live in an "emerging archipelago of self-enforced freedom and unintentional estrangement partaking in equal parts of love and death" (136), Middle-Worlders pride themselves on having "a vivid consciousness of being the Other" (149). In their case geographical coordinates locate their symbolic land because "wherever its citizens are, there the Middle World is" (147). The lack of a specific place—or for that matter, any occasional environment—is subject to unexpected changes and turns out to be a "potentially dangerous framework" (147) in which the Middle-Worlders interact and can evolve into transgressive figures subject to special narrative dynamics. In the context of the current globalized world, the Middle-Worlders are post-national figures depicted by specific images that appear with increasing frequency in contemporary written and visual narratives worldwide.

The characters in *Babel* communicate and miscommunicate. Finding themselves in a complex process of transnational negotiation they manage to (re)define themselves —and their culture—through strategies by which they respond to specific events. This transnational transaction has traits of what Randolph Bourne coined in his celebrated essay on the trans-national character of the United States of America written almost a century ago, as "cosmopolitan enterprise" (1916). The Middle-Worlder shares many common traits with the cosmopolitan person but while the cosmopolitan individual is a player of the center, the Middle-Worlder remains a peripheral figure. The cosmopolitan exhibits a kind of "internationalism, though it is more than that," Ryder claims. According to him, while internationalism values "international interaction and cooperation," cosmopolitanism—in communication and negotiations—implies much more than that since it "asks of us that we interact with others in ways that allow us to identify, and where necessary to create common interests that enable us to work together in their pursuit" (2007). For Ryder, cosmopolitanism is, on the one hand, a "guiding principle" and a "crucial component" of all transnational exchanges and, on the other hand, a way to understand each other and "ourselves in the current political and international environment" (2007); in other words it

> includes the necessity for respect for other peoples, nations, histories and cultures; a desire to move beyond one's own history and categories to attempt to understand others; a readiness to work collaboratively with others to advance shared interests and solve shared problems; a willingness at least and better an eagerness on the part of national governments, if we are to think about policy oriented cosmopolitanism, to suspend to some degree national interest as tradition-

ally understood in favor of the promotion of common interests among nations, their governments, and their people. (2007)

The Middle-Worlder is an individual who constructs a specific identity between or among cultures in a specifically tense and sometimes adverse political climate; the cosmopolitan attitude shows the ideal conditions of relationships individuals make on the cross-cultural arena, while the concept of the transnational exchange between them encompasses both a static pattern and the Dynamic Quality set composed of the individual with its intricate net of geopolitical relationships.

The fractured narrative of *Babel* shows similar conceptual traits to Richard Curtis's movie *Love Actually* (2003), a rhizomatic narrative of transnationally interlocked parallel lives that finally connects the characters under the aegis of love and trust. In terms of crisis critique *Babel* is more complex than, for example, Emir Kusturica's *Underground* (1995), which knits together war traumas, trust dilemmas and unregulated transnational relationships from within the Balkans through Europe because González Iñárritu's movie is what Roger Ebert coined as a "hyperlink film" (2007) that uproots crises of trust from specific regions or countries and places them in a set of synchronic structures with incalculable global potential. For Rafferty, *Babel* is a complex calibration of a five-day-four-story network set in different countries that are both external and internal sites of negotiations as what trust and the crisis of trust is concerned and assembled in "several apparently distinct stories that gradually reveal themselves as a single story" (2006).

The narrative launchpad of González Iñárritu's story is a desert place in Morocco. Two shepherd boys, Yussef and Ahmed (Boubker Ait El Caid and Said Tarchini) receive a rifle from their father, Abdullah (Mustapha Rachidi), who bought the gun from his neighbor Hassan (Abdelkader Bara), in order to kill the jackals that regularly decimate his goat herd. Yussef and Ahmed are living their everyday battles with life in a remote Third World village, and—as prototypes of almost-nomad Middle-Worlders—they venture into deeds where their truths no longer fit, where any previous certainties dissipate and where they, eventually, get lost. The boys start competing with each other, play with the newly bought rifle and shoot at different static and moving targets around them. Unfortunately, unlike the surrounding desert, the nearby road in the valley is not devoid of traffic: a bus full of tourists arrives when Yussef fires the gun and a random bullet hits an American passenger—Susan Jones (Cate Blanchett). This incident is the film's crucial event triggering the episodes to follow; in Pirsig's term, this is the visual point igniting the Dynamic Quality that sets local adventures and then global incidents in motion. Not fully aware of what has happened, and also very scared of the consequences of their deeds, Yussef and Ahmed quickly run away and hide the rifle while the bus speeds up toward the nearest village, where Susan is immediately helped by a caring old medicine woman and then by a veterinarian doctor, who stabilizes her condition.

Meanwhile, on the bus, an atmosphere of distrust toward local people (induced by 9/11 and its aftermath) pervades as tourists become increasingly agitated due to their fall into what Ebert sees as an "established script made of prejudice and misunderstanding" (2007). This behavior is sparked by the lingering ghost of post-9/11 terrorism, whereas in reality it was an accidental bullet that created the crisis of distrust. In the hands of Yussef, the rifle's static value has turned into a flow of Dynamic Quality. Alienated from the commodities of their assumed safe culture and frightened by the possibility of another (presumed terrorist) attack, the rest of the tourists decide to take the bus and leave the village as soon as they can, selfishly abandoning their fellow travelers: the seriously injured Susan and her husband Richard Jones (Brad Pitt), who tries to call the American Embassy for further help. The tourists of *Babel* are, in Thorstein B. Veblen's formulation, only reminders of contemporary "conspicuous consumers" (Chapter IV. "Conspicuous Consumption") behaving as media conditioned paranoids without genuine cosmopolitan features. Only Anwar (Mohamed Akhzam), the Moroccan tour guide, remains with the couple until their nightmare is over. His attitude is a model of behavior: as a local Middle-Worlder, he has genuine traits of cosmopolitanism that help him communicate and manage a problematic situation. He helps rebuild a sense of trust which was destroyed first by the gunshot and then by the fellow tourists who abandoned Susan and Richard. Despite the international turmoil upon implied political issues behind the accident that delay her transportation, Susan ultimately arrives at a hospital and recovers.

The accident, however, becomes news. The world discovers this event through the international mass media, which biased by the imminent stereotypes of the event (Morocco, local shooting, tourist bus, American woman) broadcasts it as an alleged terrorist attack. Moreover, the focus of the film turns toward a Japanese newscaster, whose report shifts the focus of the narrative from Morocco to Japan, a seemingly random move that nevertheless turns out to be significant in the course of further global investigations. According to this report,

> Susan Jones, who was wounded in a terrorist attack in Morocco, was discharged from a Casablanca hospital this morning, local time. The American people finally have a happy ending, after five days of frantic phone calls and hand wringing. (*Babel*)

The profile of the U.S. appears here both on the level of the individual and on the level of state ("American people," media, diplomacy) with special focus on the individual, who can and does genuinely transgress borders of many kinds and becomes the cosmopolitan agent of (more trustful) communication bridging over the sometimes too rigid burdens of the political reality. After the news is on the air, the government of the United States of America asks Moroccan officials to find the culprits. Following a short search on the basis of the sophisticated bullets and rifle they are quickly led to Hassan, who tells authorities that he sold the rifle to Abdullah. In the meantime, Abdullah's sons confess their deed and, in fear of retaliation, they all try to run away. But it is too late: the police start shooting at them. Finally, Ahmed is injured and Yussef surrenders, confessing the entire story that remains labeled as previously reported news. Yet, the origin of the rifle remains obscure.

Babel amasses many flashbacks, including the background story of the American couple. Susan Jones is traveling with her husband in Morocco trying to heal the loss of their child due to sudden infant death syndrome. Susan and Richard are examples of what Ryder calls "comfort" cosmopolitanists due to their behavior and simply because they "can afford it" (2007), similar to Amelia Warren's (Catherine Zeta-Jones) globetrotter-stewardess character in Steven Spielberg's *The Terminal* (2004). They trust native people not only in moments of emergency but do interact and cooperate closely with Middle-Worlders despite any crisis of trust. The Jones have two children, Debbie (Elle Fanning) and Mike (Nathan Gamble), attended in their Californian home by a Mexican nanny, Amelia (Adriana Barazza), who is impatiently waiting to attend her son's wedding in Mexico. Because of Susan's accident, Amelia has to stay in San Diego. The telephone call she receives from Richard requesting her to stay longer with the children produces the Dynamic Quality of the next narrative segment of the film. Unable to miss this important family event, she decides to take the children with her and elicits the help of her problematic nephew, Santiago (Gael García Bernal) to drive them across the border to the Mexican fiesta.

Miraculously, they cross the border without incident, enjoy the fiesta but then decide to return to the United States that night. Their Middle-Worlder status lasts only temporary; Mike is fearful of the trip. He feels, like Juan Rulfo's narrator of "Macario," that he is "passing through purgatory," (8) a feeling common to many illegal border-zone trespassers. Young Mike suffers a personal crisis of trust because he has been told that "Mexico is dangerous," to which Santiago ironically replies in Spanish that "yes, it's full of Mexicans" (*Babel*). Nevertheless, this objectification of danger leads to still another crisis of trust that occurs on the border crossing back to the United States. Here, an officer becomes suspicious of Santiago's behavior and realizes that children are traveling without a letter of consent from the parents. Confused and scared as Yussef and Ahmed were in the Moroccan scenes, Amelia decides on the spur of the moment to perform an illegal act: she crosses the border in the Tijuana desert with the Jones children. After extensive wandering in the desert—like Middle-World nomads navigating the badlands—Amelia and her charges get lost in this symbolic no man's land. The next day, afraid of possible fatal consequences, Amelia leaves the children in a place she thinks they are safe and searches for help but the border patrol finds and arrests her. The Jones children arrive home safely but Amelia is deported to Mexico after 16 years of working illegally in the United States despite the fact that Richard and Susan press no charges against her.

From Morocco, the United States and Mexico the narrative jumps to Japan, where local detectives search the source of a gun, which turns out to be the one used in the Moroccan 'attack.' While trying to find the transnational links which connect this rifle to the event in North Africa these investigators are led to Chieko Wataya (Rinko Kikuchi), a deaf-mute teenage girl living in a modern Tokyo apartment with her father, Yasujiro Wataya (Kōji Yakusho), who previously took place in a hunting trip in Morocco. Chieko is emotionally unstable; she provokes all men around her and even exposes herself naked to the detective who inquires about her father's gun. Still haunted by the tragic end of her mother who had shot herself, she tries to protect her father from any inconvenient situation and informs the detective that her mother jumped out of the window. This narrative detour encapsulates a Dynamic Quality, which is part of the strategy of her survival. Similar to Amelia's illegal border crossing (to get the children back safely) and to Yussef hiding the gun after the accident, this deaf-mute Japanese girl misleads the police about the relationship between the weapon they search for and her family members. An outcast 'othered' by her inability to communicate with both her father (about the loss of their family member) as well as with the detective she likes, Chieko starts to resemble a linguistic nomad, a Middle-Worlder, caught between her wish to communicate and her inability to do so.

Despite her confining use of sign language, Chieko is one of *Babel's* most articulate characters. She is "deaf," but "not blind" (*Babel*) and shows a desperate wish "to utter that word or sentence" but is prevented, as Ebert points out, "because of the language barrier," gender expectations, specific "cultural assumptions" and mostly by "the inability of others to comprehend" what she says or might be "actually saying" (2007). Chieko sees and understands the world around her; however, the world seems to ignore her until she finally leads the police to the story of the rifle connected to her father. Yasujiro, clarifies the situation: the gun that produced such global turmoil had once belonged to him but after a memorable hunting trip to Morocco he gave it as a gift to his local guide, Hassan. The origin of the rifle is finally solved in Japan after many transnational twists and turns and the epic of anxiety comes to a satisfactory denouement. The butterfly effect has reached its last location.

Babel tackles issues that cut across three continents, four countries, five languages (English, Arabic, Spanish, Japanese, and Japanese sign language), many nations (media) and even more people, and focuses on the vulnerability of both foreigners as tourists and natives as locals in a global climate of susceptibility. The transnational negotiations of the film take place in specific contact zones between and among certain people; these are the limits of language and culture visualized in the movie as the Moroccan desert and the windows of the tourist bus, the Tijuana border crossing and the telephone interface, the family balcony and the apartment in Tokyo and Chieko's secret notes, the screen on which the media relate the events and many more. These unrelated loci are static premises that become activated by the emergence of a small incident (a gunshot, a phone call) which causes the flow of the Dynamic Quality to spread in the region and then on a wider level, reaching even globally remote areas.

In the transnational encounters that are caused by this dynamic phenomenon, the characters of *Babel* face a series of attitudes which condition their negotiations: carelessness, paranoia, biases, stupidity, barriers of language, vulnerability and immigration issues, all placed among a crisis of trust on a global level. As Rafferty comments, in these arduous and quite abrasive conditions "when any kind of contact is achieved, against the long odds of our essential separateness," any attempt at a mutual comprehension "looks like a miracle" (2006). González Iñárritu's *Babel* discloses a few of these "miracles" in a sensible cinematic 'translation' which present the intricate articulations among global, regional, national, and local forces reflecting on complex processes of negotiations between nations, groups of people, and especially among individuals. Moreover, this "miracle" depends mostly on the individual—cosmopolitan or Middle-Worlder—that masters the crises of trust throughout the complex web of inter-personal encounters across cultures that seem to ultimately count.

Works Cited

Bourne, Randolph. (1916). "Trans-National America." Originally published in *Atlantic Monthly*, 118 (July 1916), 86-97. Web. Retrieved from: http://www.swarthmore.edu/SocSci/rbannis1/AIH19th/Bourne.html. Access: January 31, 2010.

Breytenbach, Breyten. (2009) *Notes from the Middle World. Essays.* Chicago: Haymarket Books. Print.

Cornea, Andrei. (2003). *Turnirul Khazar. Impotriva relativismului contemporan* [*The Khazar Tournament. Against Contemporary Relativism*]. Polirom, Iaşi. Print.

Cristian, Réka M. (2008). "Third Cinema Encounters." *Encounters of the Filmic Kind. Guidebook to Film Theories*. Cristian Réka M. and Zoltán Dragon. Szeged: Jate-Press, 105-122. Print.

Curtis Richard, dir. (2003). *Love Actually*. Written by Richard Curtis, Music: Craig Armstrong. Producers: Duncan Kenworthy, Tim Bevan, Eric Fellner, Debra Hayward, Lisa Chasin. Cinematography: Michael Coulter, Cast: Hugy Grant, Bill Nighy, Keira Knightley, Alan Rickman, Colin Firth, Rowan Atkinson, Emma Thompson, Martine McCutcheon, Laura Linney, Billy Bob Thornton, Liam Neeson, Martin Freeman. Distributor: Universal Pictures, Runtime: 136 minutes, Language: English. DVD.

Ebert, Roger. (2007). "Babel." *Chicago Sun Times*. September 22, 2007. Web. Retrieved from: http://rogerebert.suntimes.com/apps/pbcs.dll /article?AID=/20070922/REVIEWS08/70922001/1023. Access: January 13, 2010.

Kusturica, Emir, dir. (1995). *Underground (Once Upon a Time There was a Country)*. Writing credits: Emir Kusturica and Dušan Kovačević, Music: Goran Bregović, Cinematography: Vilko Filač, Cast: Miki Manjlović, Mirjana Joković, Lazar Ristovski, Ernst Stötzner, Dragan Nikolić, Emir Kusturica,, Srđjan Todorović, Slavko Štimac, Distributed by: New Yorker Video, Runtime: 167 minutes, Language: Serbian, English, German. DVD.

Iñárritu, Alejandro González, dir. (2006). *Babel*. Screenplay: Guillermo Arriaga, Alejandro González Iñárritu, Cast: Cate Blanchett, Brad Pitt, Adriana Barraza, Rinko Kikuchi, Gael García Bernal, Nathan Gamble, Elle Fanning, Kôji Yakusho. Distributor: Paramount Vantage, Language: English, French, Spanish, Arabic, Berber, Japanese, Japanese sign language, Runtime: 142 minutes. DVD.

Pirsig, Robert. (1992). *Lila. An Inquiry Into Morals*. London: Corgi Books. Print.

Rafferty, Terrence. (2002). "Now Playing: Auteur vs. Auteur." *The New York Times*, October 22, 2006. Web. Retrieved from: http://query.nytimes.com/gst/fullpage.html?res=9401E3D71E30F931A15753 C1A9609C8B63. Access: November 6, 2010.

Rowe, John Carlos. (2000). *Post-Nationalist American Studies*. Berkeley: University of California Press. Print.

Rulfo, Juan. (2008). *The Burning Plain and Other Stories*. Trans. George D. Schade. Austin: Univeristy of Texas Press. Print.

Ryder, John. (2007). "John Dewey, Democracy and a Cosmopolitan Ideal." *AMERICANA E-Journal of American Studies in Hungary*, Vol. III, Nr. 2, Fall 2007. Web. Retrieved from: http://americanaejournal.hu/vol3no2/ryder. Access: November 10, 2010.

Steven Speilberg, dir. (2004). *The Terminal*. Writers and Screenplay: Andrew Niccol, Sacha Grevasi, Jeff Nathanson, Music: John Williams, Cinematography: Janusz Kamiński, Cast: Tom Hanks, Catherine Zeta-Jones, Stanley Tucci, Zoe Saldana, Kumar Pallana, Berry Shabaka Henley, Diego Luna, Distributor: Dreamworks. Runtime: 128 minutes, Language: English. DVD.

Todorova, Maria. (1997). *Imagining the Balkans*. New York: Oxford University Press. Print.

Veblen, Thorstein Bunde. (2008). *The Theory of the Leisure Class* [1899]. E-Book Produced by David Reed and David Widger, Project Gutenberg. Web. Retrieved from: http://www.gutenberg.org/files/833/833-h/833-h.htm. Access: December 28, 2010.

Vianu, Lidia. (2006). *The Desperado Age. British Literature at the Start of the New Millennium* LiterNet Publishing House. Web. Retrieved from: http://editura.liternet.ro/carte/179/Lidia-Vianu/The-Desperado-Age.html. Access: December 31, 2011.

4. Afterword

Cultural Vistas and Sites of Identity: Literature, Film and American Studies discussed a number of identities in a selection of American literary texts and U.S. produced movies contextualized into the current local practice of global New American studies. The chapters of this volume presented this selection of identity sites grouped, on the basis of their primary texts, into categories of contemporary literary and filmic vistas; however, at the end, striking similitudes and intriguing analogies become visible in the complex representation of various identities appearing in the discussed range of genres and disciplines.

The book starts with the contextualization of the project within contemporary trends in American studies by placing this interdisciplinary work at the crossroads of recent several theories. Later on, the focus is on the thresholds of identity, versions of dialogic identity, on the shifting identity of the auteur and the synergic construction of the concept, on the negotiated, plural identity structured at the crossroads of cultures and art forms, and on the transnational, cosmopolitan identity.

For example, the mestiza identity in Rosario Morales's and Aurora Levins Morales's "border stories" that redefines the difference between the mainstream culture and the margins is similar to the quasi-cosmopolitan identity of the liminal Middle-Worlder characters of *Babel* handling the crisis of trust in their transnational negotiations. Moreover, the fluid identity of the protagonist in Julie Taymor's negotiated cinema presents a remarkable resemblance (as a hybrid person living between the languages and cultures of the Americas she inhabits) with the *mestiza* identity of Morales's and Levins Morales's "child of the Americas." Additionally, Frida Kahlo's plural, negotiated identity defined in *Frida* as a shift between sexualities, between her body natural and body politic, amid her conventional and unconventional way of life, between her ability and disability issues, is analogous to Edward Albee's and Paula Vogel's dramatic protagonists, who present their identity at the thresholds of the artificially built monoculture of 'normality' through their non-traditional, sometimes quite disturbing forms of relationships. Furthermore, the identity of the auteur(s) in the film adaptations of Tennessee Williams's and Edward Albee's dramas becomes flexible and stretches over intricate intradiegetic and extradiegetic realms shedding new light (besides the figure of the literary author, implied author and author-functions) on the filmic auteur-function and implied auteurship, as in the case of Williams's novel adaptations, or on the plural, synergic auteurship of the creative team in Mike Nichols's adaptation of Albee's drama.

The vistas of this volume, part of a larger project still under construction, uncover some less visible links among a heterogeneous array of identity sites pertaining to contemporary American culture, all anchored in an interdisciplinary and transnational understanding of the concept of current identities seen as malleable, shifting and dialogic "paradigm dramas" of a culture in permanent construction and open to further theoretical encounters.

www.ingramcontent.com/pod-product-compliance
Lightning Source LLC
Chambersburg PA
CBHW061747020426
42331CB00006B/1389